CHRISTIAN HEROES: THEN & NOW

HELEN ROSEVEARE

Mama Luka

Christian Heroes: Then & Now

HELEN ROSEVEARE

Mama Luka

JANET & GEOFF BENGE

YWAM Publishing is the publishing ministry of Youth With A Mission (YWAM), an international missionary organization of Christians from many denominations dedicated to presenting Jesus Christ to this generation. To this end, YWAM has focused its efforts in three main areas: (1) training and equipping believers for their part in fulfilling the Great Commission (Matthew 28:19), (2) personal evangelism, and (3) mercy ministry (medical and relief work).

To learn more about our books and materials, call (425) 771-1153 or (800) 922-2143 or email books@ywampublishing.com. Visit us online at www.ywampublishing.com.

Helen Roseveare: Mama Luka

Published by YWAM Publishing
a ministry of Youth With A Mission
P.O. Box 55787, Seattle, WA 98155-0787

ISBN 978-1-57658-910-6 (paperback)
ISBN 978-1-57658-654-9 (e-book)

Second printing 2025

Printed in the United States of America

Christian Heroes: Then & Now

Adoniram Judson
Albert Schweitzer
Amy Carmichael
Betty Greene
Brother Andrew
Cameron Townsend
Charles Mulli
Clarence Jones
Corrie ten Boom
Count Zinzendorf
C. S. Lewis
C. T. Studd
David Bussau
David Livingstone
Dietrich Bonhoeffer
D. L. Moody
Elisabeth Elliot
Eric Liddell
Florence Young
Francis Asbury
George Müller
Gladys Aylward
Helen Roseveare
Hudson Taylor
Ida Scudder
Isobel Kuhn
Jacob DeShazer
Jim Elliot
John Flynn
John Newton
John Wesley
John Williams
Jonathan Goforth
Klaus-Dieter John
Lillian Trasher
Loren Cunningham
Lottie Moon
Mary Slessor
Mildred Cable
Nate Saint
Norman Grubb
Paul Brand
Rachel Saint
Richard Wurmbrand
Rowland Bingham
Samuel Zwemer
Sundar Singh
Wilfred Grenfell
William Booth
William Carey

Available in paperback, e-book, and audiobook formats. Unit study curriculum guides are available for select biographies.

www.YWAMpublishing.com

Northern Belgian Congo
(Democratic Republic of the Congo)

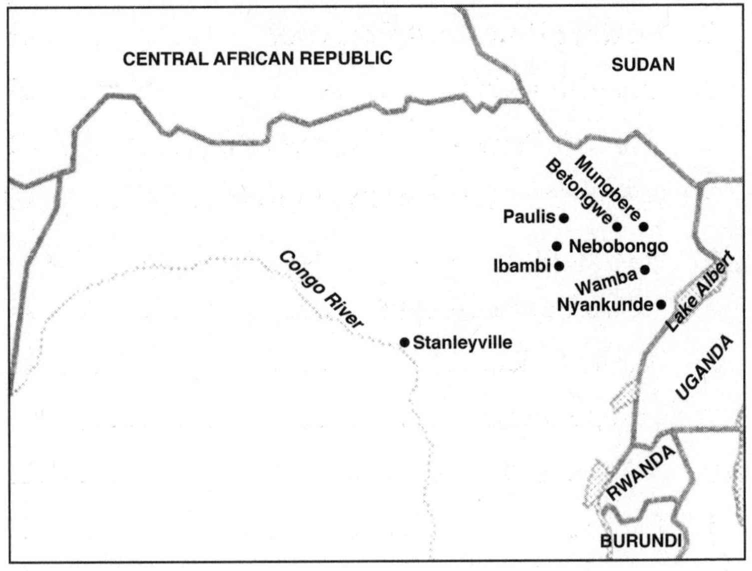

Contents

Chapter 1

It Made No Sense

News filtered into Nebobongo that the Simbas had captured the town of Paulis, about thirty miles due north. Following the takeover, three thousand people in the town who supported the national government were murdered. In the surrounding villages the Simbas conducted purges in which every man, woman, and child from a village was interrogated. Anyone who showed signs of not being one hundred percent loyal to the Simbas was killed on the spot. The same fate awaited anyone who the Simba witches felt was disloyal.

Helen recoiled at the news. How could one group of human beings do such things to another group? It made no sense. But then, this was the Republic of the Congo, where, since independence four years earlier in 1960, the country had been in political turmoil. Yet even for the Congo, with its brutal history trailing deep into the past, things had devolved to a level of lawlessness unknown to Helen and the three other missionary women working with her at the small hospital at Nebobongo in the country's north. A group calling themselves Simbas, meaning "lions" in the local Swahili language, had launched an all-out rebellion against the Congolese government. And now that rebellion was inching its way to Nebobongo.

In the following days, at times things were quiet around Nebobongo. At other times a rush of activity took place as cars and trucks filled with gun-waving youth roared past the hospital on their way to a battle. Sometimes Helen would recognize several of the cars the youth were riding in and wonder what had happened to the owners.

Before long, Simba fighters began stopping off at the hospital instead of just rolling by in the vehicles. They demanded medical treatment for sick or wounded comrades, or they rifled through all the drawers and cupboards in Helen's house, hoping to find money. They took every electrical device they could get their hands on around the hospital and taunted the medical staff, who were left without their vital, life-saving equipment.

Helen and her medical staff at Nebobongo were isolated. No one was allowed to travel or even to walk down a road without the correct papers, and the mail had ceased. Cut off from the outside world, all they could do was wait and pray that the fighting would be over soon. But Helen had a bad feeling about this rebellion. It was more brutal than any that had come before, and the killing of innocent people seemed to have reached fever pitch. She knew that one day the Simbas would come, not for medical treatment or to ransack the hospital one more time, but to take the four missionary women captive and probably kill them. A chill ran down Helen's spine at the thought. As a doctor, she'd been called to the Congo to save the lives of people like the Simba rebels who now held her life in their hands. She would never have guessed at such an outcome when she arrived in the Congo eleven years earlier.

Chapter 2

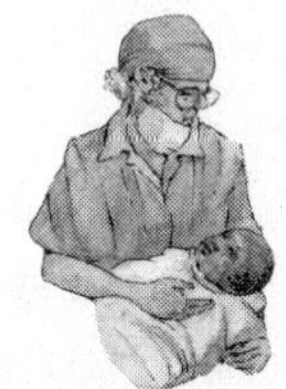

Finding Peace and Purpose

It was a cold September day in 1937 as twelve-year-old Helen Roseveare stood in the driveway of Goddington House on the outskirts of the village of Harrietsham, Kent, about thirty-five miles southeast of London. The family had recently moved into the new house, and Helen hadn't yet explored all the nooks and crannies in its many rooms or discovered where the two creeks that intersected near the front gate flowed to. She sighed. Such explorations would have to wait. Right now, Helen was off to boarding school. Beside her on the ground sat three pieces of luggage containing school uniforms, clothes for the weekends, and some of her beloved books.

As she waited for her father to bring the family car around, Helen watched her three younger sisters, Jean, Dianna, and Frances, standing on the front doorstep. Their mother, Edith, held little Frances's hand. The wheels of the car spat gravel as Martin Roseveare brought the vehicle to an abrupt halt. Helen's father loaded the luggage into the back of the car. Helen waved to her mother and sisters as she climbed into the front seat. She settled in for the 240-mile drive northwest to Denbigh in North Wales, where Howell's School was located.

Martin guided the car away from Harrietsham while Helen sat quietly watching the scenery turn from houses into rolling green fields. She knew it was a big day for her, one she would remember the rest of her life. Until now, she'd lived at home with her parents, brother, and sisters and their maid. But the car was carrying her away from all of that to boarding school, where she would spend the next six years with people she'd never met before, studying hard for an unknown future. As the car crossed into Wales, Helen felt her stomach knot. She was never comfortable around strangers. Something inside her made her feel as if everyone else knew what they were doing but she didn't. She tried to remember the advice her brother, Bob, had given her when he came home for the summer holidays. Bob was two years older than Helen and enrolled at Marlborough College, a boarding school for boys in Wiltshire. He enjoyed school life at Marlborough from the start. *But he would,* Helen thought. *Of course he would.* Bob was brilliant and funny, popular and daring, all things Helen was not.

Helen didn't mind traveling to see different things. In fact, she enjoyed it, and she knew a lot more than many girls her age. During the summer, she, her parents, her brother Bob, and her sister Jean had taken their car on the ferry from Newcastle, England, to Bergen, Norway. They had then embarked upon a camping tour of Sweden and Finland. They had even taken the train to Leningrad in the Soviet Union, where they visited the Hermitage, the largest art and cultural museum in the world. It was an impressive site.

The trip was Helen's third summer camping adventure on the European continent. The previous summer, the Roseveares had taken an equally ambitious camping trip to Istanbul, Turkey. They passed through Berlin on the way, where the Olympic Games were being held. The city was festooned in banners and flags for the occasion. The family also passed through Prague and Vienna on that trip. And in the summer of 1935, when Helen was nine, the family went to Italy, where they explored Pompeii and the Isle of Capri.

Traveling northward across Wales, Helen thought not only of the trips her family had taken but also of the home life they enjoyed. Her father worked hard as a school inspector and was often away from home during the week. Sunday, though, was when the whole family, except Bob when he was away at boarding school, were together. While Helen loved these times, she realized that going forward she would see her family only a few times a year. She wasn't even sure if she would ever live near her parents again. It was a sobering thought.

As expected, after arriving at Howell's School, Helen felt shy around the other girls. She longed to be home with her younger sisters, exploring their new house and finding cozy corners in which to sit quietly and read. Still, she pushed herself to fit in. She thought the best way to do so was to impress the other girls with her world travels. She wove involved stories about the trips, mixing fact with a lot of exaggeration. While in Berlin, she'd caught a glimpse of Adolf Hitler, Germany's chancellor, in the distance, but Helen told her fellow students she was personally introduced to him and shook his hand. When someone asked why she was singled out to meet Hitler, Helen quickly realized she needed to come up with another lie, and then another. Soon she could barely keep track of all the lies that she had told.

The depressing thing for Helen was that even with all her lively tall tales, she found it hard to make friends. She joined the drama club, even though she was afraid to speak in front of a group. The only thing Helen didn't find difficult about Howell's School was studying and passing exams. In her first year, she won the top student award in her class.

Helen returned home to Kent for the summer holidays in 1938. Before leaving, some of the other girls asked where she would be camping over the summer. Alas, there were no plans to visit the European continent this year. Although Martin Roseveare was a man of few words, when he picked his daughter up from school for the drive back to Harrietsham, Helen knew he was concerned about events happening in Europe. He told her he hoped there wasn't another war on the horizon. Helen hoped so too. Two of her uncles, her father's older brothers, had been killed twenty years ago fighting in the Great War. Her father had been shot through the stomach while serving but had survived. All summer long, Helen's father read aloud portions from the *Guardian* newspaper. He was anxious to understand whether Adolf Hitler was backing away from a fight or trying to provoke one with other countries. Instead of going to Europe during the summer, the Roseveares towed a caravan behind their car to Oxford, where they camped beside the River Thames.

Before Helen knew it, summer was over and she was back at school in Wales. This year her younger sister Jean joined her at Howell's School, easing some of Helen's homesickness. She now knew the ropes and felt she fit a little better into school life. The year passed quickly, and once again Helen won the prize for top marks in her class.

When Helen and Jean returned to their family in Kent for summer holidays in 1939, there was no talk of going anywhere to camp, not even locally. Helen's father, like so many people in Great Britain, was convinced that another war in Europe was near. Parliament in London had recently passed the Military Training Act, which ordered every young man age eighteen to twenty-one to enroll for six months of full-time military training. Helen worried about her brother Bob, who was now sixteen years old and only two years away from being called up to train for the army. She didn't know what she'd do if he was killed in a war.

By the time Helen returned to Howell's School for her third year of study, the entire country seemed shrouded in doom. Even though Wales was the farthest place in Great Britain from the European continent, the authorities ordered that every pupil at the school be issued a gas mask. Helen shuddered as she fit the clumsy, rubber contraption over her face. What would it be like to have to wear it through a wall of poisonous gas? Outside the school, and in the town of Denbigh, men and boys were busy digging ditches for residents to dive into in the event that German airplanes bombed them.

On September 3, 1939, the head mistress at Howell's School called the entire student body into the assembly hall, where she announced that Prime Minister Richard Chamberlain had just declared war on Germany. Two days before, Nazi troops had invaded Poland, one of Great Britain's allies. As a result, both Great Britain and France were now officially at war with the Germans.

Soon after war was declared, Helen's mother wrote to tell about the part her father was playing in the war effort. Martin had been transferred from his government position as a school inspector to become part of the Ministry of Food. Because he was a brilliant mathematician, his job there was to help design, implement, and oversee the rationing of food and other items across Great Britain. The Ministry of Food was located in London, and so Martin had taken a room in a boarding house in the city while he worked in his new position.

Helen's father wrote to her, explaining the importance of rationing. Seventy percent of Great Britain's food, some twenty million tons of it, was imported each year, some from as far away as New Zealand. The Germans, he noted, would surely use their warships and U-boats to try to disrupt the flow of food and starve the British people. If the Germans managed to disrupt the food supply lines, whatever food was available in the country would be shared among the population.

As Helen read her father's letter, she realized that the war was going to affect the lives of not only those who went to fight in it but all British citizens. Everyone in the country might go hungry for long periods of time. After all, the Great War had lasted four years, which seemed like an eternity to Helen.

With the start of this war, thousands of children were evacuated from the cities to Wales, particularly those located near England's east coast. Every Welsh town and village took in children, and Helen became accustomed to seeing new faces around Denbigh.

Harder to get used to than the faces of new children all over town were the blackouts. In an effort to avoid alerting German bombers at night to the location of towns and villages, all lights after dusk were banned. Heavy blankets were draped over windows in the school, and outside lights were turned off. No one drove at night because they could not use car lights. The school staff were continually checking that no glimmer of light escaped from the dormitories. Denbigh was far from any city, and Helen could only imagine what kinds of restrictions her mother and sisters were facing in Harrietsham or her father in London. Sometimes she wished she were back home in Kent, but she accepted that boarding school was the best place to get the education she needed.

The ration cards her father was involved in producing were issued in January 1940. Each person in Great Britain over the age of six received four ounces of butter, twelve ounces of sugar, and one shilling and tenpence worth of meat per week. Helen's ration was added to those of the other pupils and staff at Howell's School. A portion of the school grounds was dug up and planted with potatoes, cabbages, and brussels sprouts. Government posters with slogans like "Dig for Victory" and "Make Do and Mend" began appearing on the school noticeboards. And when Helen's class was allowed to attend a movie in town, several short films were shown before the main feature to encourage everyone to do their part to help with the war effort.

Before long, London was deemed too risky a place for such an important government department as the Ministry of Food to be headquartered. Everyone, including Helen's father, was relocated to the Welsh seaside resort of Colwyn Bay, about sixteen miles northwest of Denbigh. With their father now close by, Helen and Jean were able to visit him. On her first trip to Colwyn Bay, Helen discovered that accommodations were so scarce in the town after the influx of five thousand people from London that her father was living in a closet in his office. Such a thing would have once seemed unbelievable, but as the war dragged on, Helen found herself getting used to strange sights.

On September 7, 1940, two weeks before Helen's fifteenth birthday, the sights went from strange to haunting. On that day, almost one thousand German aircraft—over three hundred bombers escorted by six hundred fighter aircraft—crossed the English Channel and bombed London and the surrounding docks and factories. Four hundred thirty civilians were killed, and fires broke out that burned through buildings, leaving many people homeless.

Helen was home in Harrietsham, finishing her summer holiday, when the attack took place. Shortly afterward, church bells began to chime throughout the village and all over Great Britain. Edith Roseveare gathered Helen and her younger sisters into the parlor and turned on the radio. Moments later the voice of Britain's new prime minister, Winston Churchill, crackled from its speaker. Helen listened attentively as his deep voice rumbled throughout the room: "Hitler has lighted a fire which will burn with a steady and consuming flame until the last vestiges of Nazi tyranny have been burnt out of Europe." Helen wondered how long that would take, and as more German bombers attacked that night and into the next day, she decided it could be quite a while. Some of the bombers even made it as far as supposedly safe Wales, where they dropped bombs on Cardiff.

Despite the relentless bombing, life went on. A few days after the first attack, Helen and Jean boarded a bus for the trip from Kent back to Denbigh to begin the new school year. On the way, the bus passed through London, where Helen caught her first glimpse of the destruction wrought by German bombs. She saw buildings with caved-in roofs and holes in their walls. Fire smoldered in some of them while rubble was piled in the street in front of others. The smashed buildings, the rubble, the ever-present smoke, and the forlorn people standing in the midst of it all left an indelible impression of destruction and doom on her.

As the bus to Denbigh made its way along the road, suddenly air raid sirens shrieked and bombs from German airplanes overhead began to fall. Panic broke out on the street and inside the bus. Before the bus driver could bring the vehicle to a halt, several women jumped out and headed for a nearby building to take shelter. As they ran inside, a bomb crashed into the building and exploded. The bus shuddered. Helen watched in horror as the structure was immediately engulfed in flames. She could hear the women trapped inside screaming for help and watched as several Civil Defense workers came running and tried to clear an escape route from the building. But the heat of the fire and falling debris beat them back. As the building began to fall in on itself, the screams for help from the trapped women faded and then stopped.

By the time Helen made it back to Howell's School in Wales, a deep sense of hopelessness had overcome her. The destruction, the senseless loss of life—what was it all for? What was the point of being alive?

While Helen resumed her studies at school in Denbigh, the German bombing of London continued and was soon being dubbed "the Blitz." Rationing became stricter as Britain was cut off from her supply lines to Europe, North America, and beyond. All the while Helen continued with her schoolwork, but her heart wasn't in it. Everything seemed so pointless. Would England even exist when she finished school? By then, maybe Britain, like many other countries in Europe, would be occupied by the Germans or be turned into a Nazi puppet state. So many men were dying in the fighting while others were coming home maimed for life. Helen saw such men in the streets with blank faces, hobbling on crutches, a loose trouser leg dangling where a leg had once been. For her, there didn't seem to be much to live for, much to get excited about.

Sometimes Helen thought about God. It would have been strange if she didn't. Chapel was held every morning at Howell's School, but more than that, Helen's family had a long history of church work. Her father's father, who died before Helen was born, had been a canon in the Anglican Church, and two of her uncles, Richard and Edward Roseveare, were

Anglican vicars. Like her older brother and younger sisters, Helen was raised in the High Anglican tradition, though she struggled to find any real meaning in her family's religion. That is, until the summer of 1941, when some friends at school persuaded her to go with them to an SPG summer camp being held in a church hall not far from Denbigh. SPG was short for Society for the Propagation of the Gospel and was the missionary arm of the Anglican Church. Since its foundation in 1701, the society had sent out hundreds of missionaries around the world.

Helen and the other girls from Howell's School attending the SPG camp biked to the venue together. Of course, when she arrived and saw girls from different schools and churches, Helen immediately felt shy. She withdrew into herself, wondering why she'd agreed to come. But after hearing Father Charles Preston, a Franciscan monk, speak at the first daily devotional session, she changed her mind. Helen was transfixed by Father Preston, not just by his words but also by his demeanor.

Father Preston was a quiet, kind man and seemed to Helen the most sincere and serene person she'd ever met. He appeared to be unflappable despite all that was going on around him. When he spoke in the devotional sessions, his face seemed to radiate an inner light that reached out and drew Helen in.

Helen wanted what Father Preston had. She wanted to feel and care again and to know that, despite the ongoing war, she had a future. As she listened day after day during the devotional sessions,

Helen realized that what she needed was God. According to Father Preston, God was the only one who could forgive people of their wrongdoing and give them peace and fulfillment.

One afternoon Helen slipped onto her knees and poured out her heart to God. She confessed the things she'd done wrong and asked God for forgiveness. But more than that, she implored God to pour a sense of peace and purpose into her.

To her amazement, by the time she'd finished praying, she felt much better. Helen rose from prayer a different person. She began asking for forgiveness from some of the girls from Howell's School, particularly for stretching the truth in the stories she told them. And when back in Kent for the remainder of the summer, she even sought forgiveness from her parents and siblings for various things she'd said or done that came to mind.

Meanwhile, Helen's brother, Bob, had finished his secondary education and was awarded a mathematics scholarship to St. John's College, Cambridge. However, since he was now eighteen, he was forced to join the war effort. But Bob didn't go into the regular army. Instead he was recruited for top-secret work. He couldn't tell a soul, not even his parents, where he was or what he was doing. Helen wasn't surprised. Bob was particularly smart, and obviously someone high up in the military had noticed.

After summer vacation 1941, Helen continued at Howell's School. She was still shy, but she tried hard not to lie anymore. She was also able to make new friends. In fact, she became so popular that during her final year of school she was made a prefect, a student who was given special responsibilities to help the teachers run the school and keep the other students in order.

As the war years passed, the rationing system her father was in charge of became more severe. By early 1944, tea, onions, and eggs were in short supply, though Martin wrote to Helen that he was proud that they were able to offer cod liver oil and orange juice to expectant mothers and children under age five.

In spring 1944, Helen concluded her six years of study at Howell's School. She finished at the top of her class and was accepted into Newnham College, Cambridge, where she would study natural science, a prerequisite to enrolling in medical school. Because the war was still raging, Britain needed as many doctors as possible, and Helen wanted to be one. To help speed the process along, Newnham College added summer classes, enabling students to complete their natural science undergraduate degree in two years. Instead of having a summer break, Helen packed her bags and headed for the next stage in her life.

Chapter 3

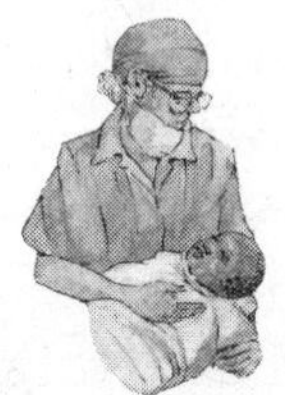

Dumbfounded

Helen and her father walked through the high, arched, red-brick entrance to Newnham College, one of two colleges at Cambridge that admitted only women. That was fine with Helen, who was there to work hard, not be distracted by young men.

Martin carried his daughter's suitcase to room 8A in Clough Hall while two attendants walked behind lugging her trunk between them. Upon reaching the room, Helen's father deposited the suitcase, kissed his daughter on the cheek, wished her well, and left. Helen looked around. Her room was small and gloomy. The windows were painted dark blue to keep the room's light from escaping outside after dark.

As Helen sat down on the bed with a thud, she felt all the excitement about this new venture draining away, leaving her lonely and full of dread. Could she handle it? She didn't know a single person at Newnham College. Would she be able to make friends? Study hard? Cope with blood? And ultimately dissect human bodies? The thought of this last question made her recoil. Was she even cut out to be a doctor? At eighteen years of age, Helen wasn't sure. Yet here she was, her worldly possessions packed in a trunk and a suitcase, ready to start a course of study that would lead to her becoming a doctor. And in the pursuit of that goal, Newnham College would be her home for the next two years.

Helen stood and reached for the straps on the trunk. Unbuckling them and opening the trunk, she began unpacking lest she change her mind about staying and bolt from the college. She piled the contents onto her bed before neatly placing her books on two small shelves attached to the wall and laying her clothes in the dresser. As she worked, Helen noticed a card tucked into the mirror frame. She pulled it out and opened it. The card read, "Hello, if you don't know anyone and have nowhere to go after supper, come and have coffee in my room, no. 12, at 8 p.m. Dorothy."

Helen felt a lump rise in her throat. Dorothy didn't even know who she was—just the girl in room 8A. What if they didn't like each other? What if Dorothy asked lots of girls to her room after supper and they all got along with each other, except for Helen? These thoughts frustrated and tormented her. Before coming to Cambridge, Helen had given herself a pep talk about being more outgoing and friendly, but her old pattern of thinking had stubbornly resurfaced.

A bell rang and Helen realized it was probably time for dinner. She poked her head out the door and saw several other students walking down the corridor. She shut her door behind her and followed them. Helen and the other girls arrived at a dining hall where, despite wartime rationing, a hearty meal was laid out to welcome the new students. In her head, Helen realized that the other new girls were in the same position. They'd come from all over the country, and some of them most likely had never been more than a few miles from home. They, too, were nervous and worried about their new environment. But telling herself this didn't stop Helen from fretting. When the girl next to her at the dinner table tried to engage her in conversation, all Helen could utter was one-word answers. The girl soon grew bored with Helen's replies and turned to talk to someone else.

Helen was so churned up inside about life at college that she didn't eat dinner that night. She stayed a respectable length of time in the dining room before pushing the plate of food aside and heading back to her room. Alone, she lay down on the bed for a short nap. She promised herself that when she awoke she'd write a letter home asking her parents to come and get her.

The clock in the courtyard was striking eight when Helen awoke from her nap. She remembered Dorothy's invitation to come for coffee and gathered the courage to go. The door of room 12 was partially open. Helen knocked and entered the room. Inside, a girl with long, black braids knelt over the hearth, poking at some crumpled, smoking newspaper. She looked up at Helen and smiled. "Do *you* know how to make a fire?" she asked with a laugh. Helen felt immediately at ease. Someone needed her help. "Let's see what I can do," she replied, reaching for another sheet of newspaper.

Soon flames blazed in the fireplace, and Dorothy hung a kettle on a dangling hook over the flames to boil water for coffee. One by one, six other girls arrived and made themselves at home on the sofa and bed in Dorothy's room. Helen was surprised at how different the atmosphere felt from dinner just three hours before. For the first time since arriving in Cambridge, she relaxed and even chatted with the other girls.

Later that night, Helen talked herself out of writing to ask her parents to come pick her up to go home. She decided that with the help of Dorothy and the other girls, she might make it through after all, that is, until her first class on Monday morning—Anatomy Dissection, a class Helen had been dreading.

As Helen walked into the laboratory, the whole place smelled of formalin. Something, but she didn't know what, was laid out under white cloths on the dissection tables. The professor introduced himself and announced that each student had a human heart to dissect. Helen recoiled. She listened to the instructions, walked to the dissection table assigned to her, propped open her textbook and picked up a scalpel.

A wave of revulsion swept over her. According to the professor, this was the first of many human organs the students would study on their way to dissecting whole cadavers. Helen took a deep breath and gingerly made the first incision. Slowly, cut by careful cut, she made her way into the heart.

As the students went about dissecting, the anatomy professor walked around the lab quizzing students on the names of various parts of the heart. Helen found this difficult. She had studied her textbook carefully the night before, but the professor's questions unnerved her and caused her to forget what she had read. Meanwhile, other students gave full answers to the professor's questions. Lessons in the Anatomy Dissection laboratory began at nine o'clock in the morning, and Helen was relieved when five o'clock arrived each afternoon and she could leave the building.

Helen looked forward to her first weekend at Newnham College and searched for some activity to be involved in. She stumbled upon the college noticeboard where someone had posted an invitation for students to join the cricket team for practice Saturday afternoon. Cricket wasn't a sport Helen played, but because she was naturally athletic she went to the practice. She was relieved to discover she wasn't the worst player who showed up.

On her first full Sunday at Cambridge, Helen looked forward to attending church. She had no doubt which church she should attend. Her entire family were High Anglicans, and she felt closest to

God during the traditional mass. Helen awoke early and walked to Little St. Mary's Church, where she found a space in a pew. She scanned the church for a familiar face, hoping that one of the other students was attending. She recognized no one. However, as the mass began, because Helen knew the words by heart, she felt at peace repeating them with the rest of the congregation.

When the service was over, Helen spoke to no one, and no one spoke to her. She hung around for a few minutes and then left, telling herself she'd probably chosen the wrong service to attend. So Helen went back for the eleven o'clock service. This time she recognized a couple of fellow students, but they were not friendly.

That night, Helen went to St. Benedict's Church, where the Franciscan monks worshiped. Following the service, she spoke to a monk and told him that she had attended an SPG summer camp in Wales at which Father Charles Preston, a fellow Franciscan monk, was one of the speakers. She earnestly explained the impact his words had had on her spiritual life. Sadly, the monk seemed uninterested in what she had to say, and Helen left St. Benedict's Church feeling depressed. She'd counted on finding a spiritual home in Cambridge, but that didn't seem likely now.

Within weeks of arriving in Cambridge, college life settled into a pattern for Helen, who, for the first time in her life, found Sundays to be her least favorite day of the week. Then about a month after being at Newnham College, Helen noticed that Dorothy and some of the other girls she had met the first night sometimes disappeared after evening study. When she asked Dorothy where they went, Dorothy replied, "We get together for a Bible study once a week. Would you like to come?"

Helen was dumbfounded—a Bible study? Why would anyone need to study the Bible? That was the job of the vicar, who would then tell members of the parish at Sunday services what they needed to know. Nonetheless, Helen's curiosity was piqued, and she agreed to attend.

The following Thursday night, Helen followed the other girls from study hall. Each girl carried a Bible, and once they all sat down, one of the girls instructed the others to open their Bibles to Ephesians chapter three. Helen hadn't thought to bring a Bible with her. The truth was, she didn't own one. She looked on as the girls took turns reading aloud a few verses each from the book of Ephesians. When they finished reading, Helen listened as they began discussing the meaning of the passage and how they could apply it to their daily lives. Helen was amazed. She'd never thought of reading and discussing the Bible in this way.

The next Sunday after a late dinner, Dorothy invited Helen to go with her to a Christian meeting on campus. Helen agreed and found herself at the Cambridge Inter-Collegiate Christian Union (CICCU), or CU for short. Several hundred Cambridge students were in attendance, all listening intently to the sermon. Again, Helen was challenged by the experience. There was none of the ritual of her High Anglican church—no incense, no rote prayers, no responsive readings, no men wearing crisp, white vestments. But there was something simple and lively about this meeting and those attending it.

Bit by bit, Helen was drawn into Dorothy's circle of Christian activity. She enjoyed the sense of belonging and the new friendships she was developing. By the end of her first term at Newnham College, Helen hardly wanted to go home to see her family. Her parents had recently moved from Harrietsham, Kent, into a new home in southeast London. For the first time since the war began, they were back living together in the same house with Helen's younger sisters. By now, Martin had been ordered back to work with the Ministry of Education, where he was appointed Chief Inspector of Schools for Great Britain. It was because of his new position that the family had moved to London.

Helen found it hard fitting in with her family after a term at university. She felt so much more mature than her sisters, and Bob was still away and busy with his top-secret work for the war effort.

While life in Great Britain remained grim, the war had entered a new phase. On June 6, 1944, 155,000 British and Allied troops crossed the English Channel and landed on the beaches of Normandy, determined to liberate France from the Germans. Hitler retaliated by using a secret weapon, the V1 flying bomb, nicknamed the Doodlebug, to attack Great Britain. The weapon was unlike anything the world had ever seen—a self-propelled missile that could be launched from the ground rather than having to be dropped from an aircraft. Many people in the south of England felt hopeless as over a hundred missiles a day were fired from Nazi sites in France, Belgium, and Holland. Not only had these V1 flying bombs killed thousands of people, but also they had destroyed over 200,000 homes along with train stations, power stations, and bridges. Despite these attacks, the Allied invasion of France pressed ahead, causing German forces to pull back or risk being overrun.

Helen returned to university for her second term with Doodlebugs on her mind. She could hear them whizzing overhead at night. This was a mixed blessing. If she heard them, she knew she was safe. But each Doodlebug that missed them was going to hit some other target and wreak havoc. Helen was glad to get back to her friends. She soon slipped into the habit of attending Bible study and Cambridge CU prayer meetings. Since everyone else seemed to know the Bible better than Helen, she borrowed a copy from the college library and began reading the New Testament.

At the same time, Helen was asked to try out for the Newnham College hockey team. Her brother, Bob, was an avid hockey player, but Helen had never tried the game. Nonetheless, she excelled at goalkeeping and was made team goalkeeper. In fact, she did so well in the position that within weeks she was also made goalkeeper for the Cambridge University women's hockey team. The captain of this team was Olga Rutherford, who also attended Newnham and was a year ahead of Helen in her studies. Olga was studying chemistry, but she was also the outspoken leader of the Women's Communist Party at the university. She invited Helen to party meetings to hear lectures on how the Soviet Union was Great Britain's ally in the war and how the best way to win against Nazi Germany was for Britain to become a socialist state like the Soviet Union. Olga also railed against the upper classes in England. Helen understood why when Olga described her grim background growing up in a coal-mining town in the north of England.

Helen soon found her Sundays divided into three parts. She would first attend morning mass at the Anglican church, then Communist rallies and meetings in the afternoon, and CU prayer meetings in the evening. It seemed an odd combination to many, but Helen felt invigorated by it.

As Christmas approached, Helen's mother wrote to say it was best if she didn't come home for the holiday. Her sister Dianna had the mumps and was under quarantine. Helen scrambled to find somewhere else to go. Two of her friends offered their homes for a week each, leaving Helen with nowhere to go for the last ten days of the holiday break. Dorothy and another friend, Sylvia, arranged for Helen to attend a "house party," or Christian retreat, at Mount Hermon Bible College.

On December 27, 1944, Helen found herself on a train bound for Ealing in West London, where Mount

Hermon Bible College was located. As soon as she arrived, she felt out of place. All the other women in the group were enthusiastic Christians who had gathered to learn how to set up and lead local Christian mission activities. Helen certainly didn't feel like doing that. She was comfortable with her private Anglican faith. However, just as she'd been at the Newnham College Bible study, Helen was so impressed with how much these other women knew about the Bible that she purchased her first Bible and began studying the Book of Romans along with the other women.

For some reason during the house party, Helen found herself getting grumpier as time went on. While the others talked about the love and joy of Jesus Christ, Helen preferred to talk about specific Christian doctrines that Anglicans held and others did not. This led to a vigorous argument at dinner on the last night, causing Helen to leave the dinner table in tears. She ran upstairs and flung herself onto her bed. What was wrong with her? Why did she care so much about petty issues? Why didn't she have the same peace and joy the other women had? Why did she want to argue all the time? As she lay pondering these questions, Helen realized that she was afraid to let go of her Anglican ideals and truly accept others who belonged to different church groups. Constantly evaluating others to see how their beliefs differed from hers had made her judgmental and argumentative.

Loneliness and a feeling of failure engulfed Helen. Would she ever be able to live up to the Christian ideals she'd set for herself? How did the other women seem to do it so effortlessly? She prayed, asking God to help her understand. She then looked up at the picture hanging on the opposite wall of a bunch of roses with the words "Be still and know that I am God" written beneath in bold black type. At once Helen felt peace and joy flood through her. She knew her Christian faith didn't depend upon her hard work or her ability to win arguments. All that was required of her was to be still and know that God was at work. Helen felt as if a great weight had been lifted from her. She was free to love, free to stop judging others, free to let God deal with other people's faults. All she had to do was be still. It made perfect sense to her. She got up from her bed, washed her face, and headed back downstairs. She felt as if she were walking on air.

Downstairs the final meeting of the house party was about to take place in the sitting room. Helen joined the others as the leader opened the meeting with an opportunity for anyone to give her testimony. Helen wasn't sure what that meant, and so she sat silently with the others. The leader tried again, "Would anyone like to share with us what God has done for them this week?"

Now Helen understood what she was being asked. She raised her hand and opened her mouth to speak. But what could she say? How could she describe what had just happened to her? No words came out. Her mind was blank. After what seemed like an eternity, she blurted, "I've encountered God here, and I know He has forgiven me, and . . .

and . . ." Because she couldn't think of anything else that needed to be said, she ended with "and that's all" and then sat down.

The woman next to Helen leaned over and whispered, "I knew something had happened to you. Your face was shining when you came down those stairs."

Helen smiled and nodded. She wasn't surprised. She felt like a brand-new person inside as she snuggled into her chair, ready to hear the main speaker, the Reverend Graham Scroggie, preach one last time.

Following the meeting, Helen spoke with the Reverend Scroggie, who asked if he could write something on the flyleaf of Helen's new Bible. Helen handed her Bible to him, and he wrote "Philippians 3:10." Handing the Bible back, he looked directly into Helen's eyes and said, "Tonight you've entered into the first part of the verse, '*That I may know him.*' This is only the beginning, and there's a long journey ahead of you. My prayer for you is that you will go on through the verse to know '*the power of his resurrection*' and also, God willing, one day perhaps, '*the fellowship of his sufferings, being made conformable unto his death.*'"

Helen thanked the reverend, but in her heart, she wondered what kind of encouragement in the faith it really was. She certainly wasn't enthusiastic about the suffering part.

Chapter 4

"I Don't Believe . . . I Know Him"

Helen's next year at Cambridge was wonderful. She joined in all kinds of Christian meetings, began a four-year Bible study correspondence course, and joined the InterVarsity Missionary Fellowship. She spent an hour each morning reading her Bible, taking notes, and memorizing Scripture. As she read and studied, she was often surprised when stories familiar to her since childhood now seemed to jump off the page, infused with new meaning for her daily life.

Helen also continued playing sports: hockey in winter and cricket in summer. Her friendship with Olga continued despite Olga's strong communist views. During the summer of 1945, Helen helped lead a teenage girls camp in Chulmleigh, Devon. While there, on August 14, 1945, church and clock tower bells rang out all over Great Britain, celebrating victory over Japan. The war was over. Three months before, on May 7, Nazi Germany had surrendered to the Allies, ending the fighting in Europe. And now, following the dropping of two atomic bombs on Japan by the Americans, Japan's emperor had surrendered to the Allies.

Helen could hardly believe it. Great Britain had been in the grip of war for six long years, from the start of her third year of study at Howell's School in Wales. Everyone at camp joined the Chulmleigh locals as they held a thanksgiving service. As Helen sang the final hymn at the service, she thought of all of the opportunities ahead. She would no longer be called up to join the war effort when she graduated from medical school. She was free to make her own decisions about her future.

On January 1, 1946, Helen was delighted to learn that her father was included on the king's New Year Honours list of men and women who had made significant contributions to society in England and throughout the British Empire. Her father was recognized for his work organizing and managing the difficult and ever-changing rationing system. For his efforts, he was knighted by the king, and going forward, Helen's parents would be addressed as Sir Martin and Lady Edith Roseveare.

The rest of the school year passed quickly. Helen continued her premedical studies, her Christian activities, and her involvement in sports. Toward the end of term, the Cambridge University Women's hockey team, for which Helen continued to play, traveled to Clacton, fifty miles to the southeast beside the sea, to participate in a hockey tournament. Olga was still team captain, and Jessie, another Newnham College student, was also on the team. In Clacton, the three girls ended up sharing an attic room at the Girls' Friendly Society Hostel. The first night there, when the light was turned out, Helen debated whether she should get down on her knees to pray before sleeping or, if God wouldn't object, just pray silently in bed. After a brief battle with her pride, Helen slipped out of bed and onto her knees, where she quietly prayed while Olga and Jessie remained silent. When Helen got back into bed, Olga asked in a mocking voice, "What was the point of that? Prayer doesn't change anything. It just makes you look foolish."

Helen gulped. "It's one way I stay connected to God," she replied.

Olga laughed. "Do you really think God, if there is one, listens to your prayers? Right here? Right now? Isn't it much more practical to take action like communists are taught to do? We don't wait for God. We get in and make the world a fairer place."

"Well," Helen replied, staring at the stars through the attic window, "that's not how I see it."

Olga and Helen talked into the night about the differences between Christianity and communism. They continued talking on the way to games, between games, and during meals, but nothing Helen said seemed to make a difference. Olga was sure there was no God and that it was up to people to make the world around them a better place. Helen found her hard to argue with. Sometimes she didn't have an answer for Olga's questions and found it easier to say so. "I don't have an answer for that," she told Olga several times, "but I do know that Jesus Christ, God's Son, came to this earth to die on the cross to reconcile you to God and that He rose again."

"But how can you believe that?" Olga would challenge her over and over.

"I don't *believe* in Jesus . . . I *know* Him," Helen would reply. "There is a difference. Once you know someone, you can't deny he exists, can you?"

Jessie listened quietly to the backward and forward of their conversation, and when they returned to Cambridge, she attended CU meetings with Helen. After several weeks, she declared she'd become a Christian too. Helen was greatly encouraged by this, especially since Olga had appeared to want less to do with her and her Christian friends.

In spring 1947, Olga graduated from Newnham College but returned to work in the college's chemistry department. Helen learned that she was staying in a room in a rundown apartment, cooking her meals over a single burner.

Every three years the Cambridge Inter-Collegiate Christian Union held a university-wide outreach they called a crusade. Helen became a member of the organizing committee for the upcoming 1947 crusade. The committee invited Dr. Donald Barnhouse, a pastor and radio host from the United States, to be guest speaker at the crusade. As Helen planned the events, she longed to ask Olga to come along and hear Dr. Barnhouse speak, but it didn't seem likely that Olga would take her up on the invitation. Then, out of the blue, Olga knocked on Helen's dorm room door. She wanted to borrow some hockey gear. Helen was encouraged. Was this the opening she'd been praying for? Later that night, when Olga returned the equipment, Helen invited her to stay for a hot bath. She knew it would be appreciated, since there was a massive coal shortage in England, and hot water was a precious commodity. Olga agreed. While her friend bathed, Helen made her supper and prayed that God would speak to Olga's heart.

A few days later, Helen went to the chemistry department to invite Olga to the crusade meeting. Olga made an excuse as to why she couldn't go, but Helen said she would stop in at the lab on the way to the meeting in case Olga changed her mind. When Helen returned to the chemistry department on her way to the meeting, Olga was still there and agreed to go with her to the event.

Donald Barnhouse was an imposing figure with a strong voice and twangy American accent. He preached about how God requires humans to be sinless and how that is impossible without the grace of God. He raised his hands. "One hand is the judgment of God," he said, clenching one fist. "The other hand is the forgiveness of God through the death of Jesus Christ." As he spoke he opened the other hand. Then he added, "The only way to come to God is through Jesus Christ. If you have the slightest desire to do that, stand with me and let us pray."

Helen felt a rustle beside her. She turned to see Olga standing!

After the service Helen hugged Olga. "I don't feel any different," Olga told her matter-of-factly. "You told me if I believed I would know. To the best of my ability, I've believed, but I do not know. If I don't know anything in the next few days, I'll consider this an experiment in proving you wrong, and I will have no further interest in Jesus Christ."

Helen took this as a gauntlet thrown down. She asked all her Christian friends to pray for Olga, and she made sure Olga came to every one of Dr. Barnhouse's meetings. Olga was never far from Helen's thoughts. Helen prayed for her wherever she was, skipping meals and losing sleep to do so. At the end of the week, Olga turned to Helen and told her that she now knew in her heart that Jesus Christ was real and that He had saved her.

It was the news Helen had been longing to hear. Excitedly she introduced Olga to the Scripture Union method of reading through the Bible, and the two of them often met to discuss Christian themes and to pray together.

About a month after the crusade, Helen heard a knock at her dorm room door. She opened it to discover Princess Aida Desta of Ethiopia, a first-year student at Newnham College. Helen had been asked by the school matron to take Aida under her wing.

Aida was the eldest granddaughter of Emperor Haile Selassie of Ethiopia. Her mother and sisters had fled into exile in England in the 1930s after Italy had invaded their country. Princess Aida told Helen that the matron of her previous boarding school, Clarendon Girls' School, where her younger sisters still attended, was urgently looking to fill the job of assistant matron. Helen and Aida knelt and prayed that God would supply someone to fill the position. No sooner had the two women finished praying than there was another knock at the door. Olga came rushing in. "I've quit my job," she declared breathlessly.

"Why?" Helen asked.

"As you know, I'm working on research involving war weapons. As a Christian, I don't think I can do that anymore."

"What do you think God wants you to do next?" Helen asked.

"I'm not sure. Pray for me that God will show me what He wants me to do next. In the long term, I think I've been called to be a missionary." The news startled Helen. "I need a job where I can work out my Christian faith," Olga continued, plopping herself onto Helen's bed.

"Have you ever heard of Clarendon Girls' School?" Helen asked.

Within ten minutes, Helen was on the telephone to the matron at Clarendon Girls' School. Several days later, Olga packed her bags, left Cambridge, and headed to Clarendon. It had all happened so quickly. Helen barely had time to think it through, though she was sure that God had His hand on the whole venture.

In July 1947, Helen graduated from Newnham College with a natural science degree with second-class honors. She was twenty-one years old and ready to begin the next phase of her life, studying as a medical student at West London Hospital. But first, Helen had a family celebration to attend. Helen's older brother, Bob, had graduated from St. John's College, Cambridge, with a degree in mathematics. He was due to marry Ione Jay on August 7. Although the Roseveare family knew that Bob had met Ione at work, that work was still classified as top secret, and no one knew what the two of them had been doing.

Helen's younger sisters were growing up fast. Jean was twenty and had followed Helen's footsteps to Newnham College. The two other sisters, fourteen-year-old Dianna and twelve-year-old Frances, seemed interested in becoming teachers, like their father.

Following Bob and Ione's wedding, Helen made her way to West London Hospital, where other graduates warned her to be prepared—her university study in Cambridge had been easy compared to what lay ahead.

Chapter 5

Repair the House of the Lord

West London Hospital was about twelve miles from the Roseveare home in Bromley. Helen decided to live at home and commute each day by bus. Life at West London Hospital soon fell into a pattern of visiting wards with teaching physicians, listening to lectures, and attending study hall. Helen's busy life was very different from that of being a student at Newnham College. It made Helen realize how much spare time she'd had at Cambridge to go to Christian meetings and enjoy time with friends. In London, the only time she was away from her studies was Saturday afternoon and Sunday. Helen decided to make the most of this time by teaching a Girl Crusader Union class in the garage of her parents' house on Sunday afternoons. She enjoyed talking with younger girls, encouraging them in their faith, and searching the Bible with them for answers. The girls seemed to enjoy their time with Helen, because before long they were meeting with her on Saturday afternoons too.

Although there was no Christian fellowship group at West London Hospital, Helen did what she could. She got permission from the hospital board, the matron, and the chaplain to conduct informal services in the wards on Sunday mornings. These were simple affairs, and at first Helen was often the only student who showed up. Helen lugged a portable harmonium from ward to ward although she didn't really play the instrument. After handing out hymn sheets, she would tap out the tune with two fingers on the keyboard. Sometimes the patients appreciated her effort and hummed or sang along. At other times, they did not. During the first service Helen held in the men's orthopedic ward, one young man threw a boot at her. It landed on the harmonium, surprising Helen, who managed to keep tapping out the tune. When the hymn was over, she picked up the boot and hurled it back at the man who threw it. The other young men in the ward clapped and cheered. Helen smiled. The men didn't know she'd bowled for the Cambridge women's cricket team. The men of the ward settled down after that and looked forward to Helen's visits. During each service, Helen preached the gospel for a few minutes. Much to her surprise, one patient became a Christian as a result.

At the beginning of 1948 another large family gathering was held. It was a farewell to Bob, Ione, and baby Richard, who were leaving for South Africa. While on a university hockey tour of the country, Bob was offered and accepted a job teaching mathematics in a boys' boarding school in Natal. Although Helen was happy for her brother, she found it hard to say good-bye to him. She and Bob had always been close.

Later in 1948, Helen attended a different type of gathering: a movie documentary titled *Three Miles High,* which had been filmed in technicolor by Major Leonard Moules. Although weary from a long day working in the emergency ward, Helen and a nurse friend caught a train to Richmond to see the movie. They arrived late, found the theater packed, and had to stand outside the door at the back. From there it was hard to see, and the two of them took turns standing in front of each other for a better view. What Helen saw and heard of the movie stirred her heart. The documentary, which had been filmed along the border of North India and Tibet, was about the work that Worldwide Evangelization Crusade (WEC) missionaries had been carrying out in that area over the previous twenty years. Helen recalled that WEC had been founded by C.T. Studd, the famous cricket player from Cambridge University who left fame and fortune behind in England in February 1885. C.T. and six other young men from Cambridge had traveled to China to serve as missionaries with China Inland Mission. The group became known as the Cambridge Seven. Ultimately C.T. made his way to Africa, where he served as a missionary until his death in 1931. While living in Africa, he founded WEC, which now, in 1948, remained a flourishing mission.

When the movie was over, the crowd slowly dissipated, but Helen stayed behind. She wanted to talk to Major Moules, who had introduced the film and was now manning the WEC book table at the back of the theater. She had a million questions for him: How did he know he'd been called to missions? What was it like being a missionary? Was there a need for medical missionaries in Tibet?

After Helen introduced herself to Major Moules, the major did his best to answer her questions, and each of his answers challenged her. She explained her desire to serve God and how, after learning that her friend Olga had felt God call her to become a missionary, she also thought she was feeling a call to missionary service, though she wasn't sure where. Major Moules invited Helen to visit him and his wife, Iris, at the WEC headquarters in London's Upper Norwood neighborhood. Helen eagerly took his card with the headquarters address on it.

As she rode the train and then the bus home that night, Helen had a feeling something life-changing had just occurred. And it had. When she visited WEC headquarters a week later, she was overwhelmed by the sense of purpose that everyone living there seemed to have. The headquarters consisted of four houses located together on Highland Road. The one Helen visited at 19 Highland Road was a large hostel building that stood next door to the home in which

C.T. Studd and his family had once lived. In fact, it had been built on the site where the stables for the Studd house had once sat. The three-story, red-brick hostel housed thirty people and included a dining room that could be quickly transformed into a meeting room for one hundred people. The whole operation was impressive, but Helen was even more impressed with the people who greeted her. Among those staying in the building, in addition to Major Leonard Moules; his wife, Iris; and his sister-in-law Edith, his brother's widow, were a number of missionaries home on furlough. From them Helen learned that as a mission, WEC was growing fast. Following the death of C.T. Studd in 1931, Norman Grubb, C.T.'s son-in-law, took over guiding the ministry. Under Norman's leadership WEC had grown from about thirty-five missionaries working mostly in Africa to several hundred missionaries working in scores of countries around the world.

Given the friendly atmosphere at the WEC headquarters, Helen gladly accepted Major Moules's invitation to stay for dinner. Along with the furloughing missionaries, several young men and women were staying in the house and attending Bible colleges nearby, and the dinner talk centered around Christian things. It was the kind of conversation Helen had missed since leaving Cambridge.

Following her first visit, Helen had an open invitation to return for dinner at WEC headquarters anytime she wanted, and she was soon a regular visitor.

On March 5, 1949, Helen's sister Jean married a

decorated war hero, Captain John Ross. They were both medical students. John was training at West London Hospital, though he and Helen were in different classes. Helen's brother, Bob, his wife, Ione, and their son, Robert, returned from South Africa to attend the wedding.

With two of her siblings married, Helen began to wonder whether marriage was somewhere in her future.

By now Norman Grubb and his wife, Pauline, had returned from a long overseas speaking trip and were living in the Studd house at WEC headquarters. Four months after Jean and John's marriage, Norman Grubb approached Helen and asked if she would consider coming to live at WEC headquarters to help take care of Major Moules's sister-in-law Edith, who had been a nurse in the Congo. Edith had been diagnosed with cancer a few months before, and it was now difficult for her to get out of bed. Helen agreed, and for the next six weeks she oversaw Edith Moules's medical care. Forty-nine-year-old Edith had lost her husband to typhoid fever in Africa. Although she knew she would die soon, she spent every spare moment praying for the mission work among those with leprosy in the Congo. She told Helen about the start of her missionary journey, how at age twenty-seven she had gone to the Congo and stayed at Ibambi, where C.T. Studd lay ill and weak in his hut.

"I found the old man," Edith said, "living in a bamboo house with a mud floor, a wood fire burning in the middle, a few shelves around the walls with his boxes and some bottles and tins, and a rough bed and blankets in the corner. Every night the missionaries gathered around his bed—I remember it like yesterday—and he would read the Bible and teach from it. Hardly a night went by when he didn't throw out the challenge 'If Jesus Christ be God and died for me, then no sacrifice can be too great to make for Him. This is the only way the dying world can be won!'"

"Those were thrilling days!" Edith went on. "But the conditions were tough, and we were dealing with a very primitive Africa in those days. There were no doctors, few nurses, and no medical workers within miles and miles. In fact, none had been thought of. People were brought to me tied to a pole carried between two men. Sometimes they arrived on the backs of their relatives, anywhere from twenty, thirty, even forty miles away. It was a great joy to serve them. I was thrilled to be able to care for them and talk to them a little about the Lord."

During the time they had together, Helen learned from Edith how she had resisted at first working with lepers, but how God had convicted her that lepers, too, were her neighbors. So, in 1940, a thriving leper community began at Nebobongo, about seven miles from Ibambi.

"You have to let go of everything, your expectations, your right to use your expertise, your right to be in charge—all such things—if you want to really be used by God. That's the main thing I'd tell you," Edith said to Helen one day. "I always think back to a story Mr. Harrison, a missionary, used to tell about an African man who came to him for help. The man had a terribly mutilated hand, dripping with blood. It was cut across the palm in a dozen places. Mr. Harrison dressed and bandaged the wounded hand and then asked how the man got such an unusual injury.

"'I had my arrows in my hand, and someone tried to take them from me,' the man told him. 'Why didn't you let them go?' Mr. Harrison asked. 'Because they were my arrows,' said the man. In the same way, I had to let go, and you will too, Helen. Even if you have ownership, or you are right, you have to trust God to engineer things at the other end. There are always two sides to every situation, of course, but it doesn't matter whether the other side is 100 percent right or 100 percent wrong. It is my own attitude that I have to account to God for."

Helen wondered why Edith had taken the time to tell her this. Did Edith see some difficulties ahead for Helen?

Edith died on September 6, six weeks after Helen had moved into WEC headquarters. A memorial service was held for her in Westminster Chapel, and eight hundred people attended. As she sat through the service, Helen thought about how grateful she was to have had the opportunity to get to know Edith before her death.

After the memorial service, Helen continued to live at WEC headquarters. It felt like the right thing to do. Not only was the headquarters closer to West London Hospital than the Roseveare home in Bromley, but also Helen was energized by the fellowship of other mission-minded Christians.

After working hard to pass her exams and having to retake one of them, Helen graduated with a medical degree at Christmastime 1949. Now a qualified doctor, she felt it was time to take the next step toward her goal of becoming a missionary. Normally this would have been to attend Bible college for two or three years before applying to WEC for an overseas post. But so much of Helen's life had not been normal. She had lived in community since starting boarding school in Wales at age twelve, and she had been living at WEC headquarters for the past six months, fully joining in the life of the mission.

Helen had also completed the Bible correspondence study course she had begun four years earlier. This alone was an impressive accomplishment, one the mission leadership took into account when they allowed Helen to skip the Bible college requirement for entry into the mission. Instead, they asked her to continue living at the headquarters until she had a clear understanding of where she thought God was calling her. This soon became a problem. Just about every missionary outreach wanted a doctor to join it. In many areas of the world where WEC missionaries served, there were no Western medical professionals, and although all WEC workers undertook basic first aid and midwife courses, having a qualified doctor on staff was a tremendous asset. Helen didn't know where she was called to go, but she knew where she didn't want to go—anywhere missionaries had already established a base of operation. She wanted to go where she would have to pioneer a new ministry and a new mission base.

One Tuesday in April 1950, Helen was dusting the dining room, as she often did. On a shelf sat a calendar pad with a Bible verse for each day of the year printed on it. She noted that the day's verse was 2 Chronicles 24:4: "And it came to pass after this, that Joash was minded to repair the house of the LORD." The phrase "repair the house of the LORD" seemed to jump out at Helen. Without thinking, she tore off the calendar page and slipped it into her pocket.

Two days later, Helen received a letter from an old school friend, who, unbeknownst to her, had become a Christian. After explaining her conversion, the friend wrote that she'd felt impressed by God to send a Bible verse to Helen. To Helen's great surprise it was the same verse as on the calendar page in her pocket—2 Chronicles 24:4. Helen's interest was roused. What could it mean? She looked up the verse in the Bible and read the verses before and after it, but nothing in particular came to mind.

The following morning Helen, along with everyone else living at the headquarters, attended prayers. The leader of WEC's leprosy crusade led the meeting and explained how burdened she was for the mission's work in the Congo. "Over fifteen hundred leprosy patients are in our care, and over a quarter of a million people look to us for medical care along with spiritual help and education. It grieves me that after thirty years of pioneer work, we still have no doctor to offer them. When I read this from 2 Chronicles 24:4, on Tuesday's calendar, "repair the house of the Lord," I became sure that our mission is called to send qualified medical missionaries to the Congo to repair the breach in the wall—the hole that has been there for thirty years waiting for someone to fill it."

Helen felt her heart pounding as she heard the verse for the third time in less than a week. This time, though, the speaker had linked the verse to the need for medical staff in the Congo. *It's just too bad it's the Congo,* Helen thought to herself as she tried to dismiss the notion. She wanted to go to people who'd never before encountered missionaries or heard the gospel, not to a mission station that had been operating since the beginning of WEC.

As Helen returned home to visit her family that weekend, she prayed that God would somehow make it clear to her if indeed she was to go to the Congo. At church on Sunday morning, the vicar read the story from the Bible about Balaam and his donkey. He went on to speak about God's call on a person's life. "Three times the Lord has clearly spoken to you," the vicar said, "but you do not want to heed. You want something special and dramatic. Beware! He may not be patient forever. Heed His voice in the message He has repeated to you three times and obey—and He will bless you."

Helen was stunned. She had been presented with the same verse three times. She had listened as a WEC leader linked repairing the breach in the wall to the mission's work in the Congo. Now the vicar had read how God had spoken to Balaam though his donkey three times and expected him to obey. Somewhere, deep in her heart, the matter was settled for Helen.

She surrendered her dream of heading out into some unknown part of the world and embraced the call to be a doctor in the Congo.

Helen was greatly relieved to know where she would be going as a missionary. Now it was time to prepare. One of the first things she needed to prepare for was language. French was one of the official languages of Belgium, the Congo's colonial overlord. It was also the official language of the Congo, and Helen did not speak it.

She also tried to learn as much about the history of the Congo as possible. For many years the Congo River Basin remained unexplored by European colonial powers. The area encompassed by the basin consisted of broad expanses of jungle where all manner of tropical diseases, which could kill an unsuspecting European in a matter of hours or days, ran rampant. In 1885 King Leopold II of Belgium claimed the area as his own private state, calling it the Congo Free State. However, his drive to economically exploit the area proved disastrous. He brutalized the Congolese people and set in place ruthless officials to keep law and order. The ensuing violence and poverty this created led to the Belgian government taking official control of the country in 1908, creating the Belgian Congo. Since then the Belgian government had done a lot to streamline and improve the colonial administration of the country. Yet there was still so much to be done for the Congolese people, especially in rural areas. To help meet these needs, the Belgians turned to mission and humanitarian organizations for assistance.

As part of her preparation for the Congo, in September 1951 Helen made her way to Brussels, the Belgian capital, where she stayed at the Colonial School and studied French under the stern eye of Professor Gilsoux. She hoped that after five months of concentrated language study she would know enough to retake her medical exams in French, something required for any doctor working in the Congo.

Sure enough, Helen's grasp of the language after five months of study was sufficient to pass her medical exams in French. After passing the exams, she moved to Antwerp, Belgium, where she spent four months studying tropical medicine and hygiene. During this time she learned things she had never thought of before: how to identify deadly snakes and symptoms of various diseases and illnesses, how to treat the damage done to the human body by the abundance of parasites and worms in the region, and how to keep herself as safe as possible from contracting various diseases.

By May 1952, Helen was back in England. She spoke passable French and now had a diploma in tropical medicine and hygiene. She took a break to be with her family before embarking upon the next phase of her preparations—raising the money she would need for her personal support on the mission field. To do this, Helen was paired with Nellie Stokes, a WEC missionary who'd had to leave her work in China because of the Communist Revolution there. For six months Helen and Nellie traveled from town to town around the United Kingdom raising money from individual Christians and churches to fund the missionary work they were about to undertake.

When she returned to WEC headquarters in London, Helen had a lot to do: purchase, pack, and label supplies and clothes; visit shipping agents; and obtain visas and permits. When all the preparations had been made, on February 13, 1953, twenty-seven-year-old Dr. Helen Roseveare, a one-way ticket in her hand, boarded the steamship *Dunnottar Castle* in London. The ship was bound for Mombasa, Kenya, in East Africa, the first leg of her journey to the Congo.

Chapter 6

Their Child

As the *Dunnottar Castle* sailed from England, Helen was able to relax for the first time in weeks. The bustle of preparation was behind her, her luggage was stowed in the ship's hold, and a packet of visas and permits sat on the side table in her cabin. Over the next three weeks the ship would sail down the coasts of France, Spain, and Portugal, through the Strait of Gibraltar, across the Mediterranean Sea, through the Suez Canal, and on to Mombasa. Traveling with Helen on the *Dunnottar Castle* were several WEC missionary couples. The Robertses and the Greens were returning to their mission stations following furlough in England, and the Butters, an American couple, were undertaking a tour of WEC's work in the Congo.

As the ship steamed south, the missionaries aboard met each morning for prayer and Bible study, followed by two hours of language study. After five months of concentrated French language study in Brussels, Helen was now learning Swahili, the dominant language spoken throughout the area where she would be working.

After passing through the Strait of Gibraltar, the *Dunnottar Castle* headed to Genoa, Italy. After a stop there it headed across the Mediterranean to Egypt and entered the Suez Canal at Port Said. After traversing the canal, the ship sailed down the Gulf of Suez and across the Red Sea to Aden, where they made a stop. From Aden they rounded the Horn of Africa and sailed south down the east coast of the continent until docking in Mombasa. As the journey progressed, Helen began noticing that the farther south the ship traveled, the higher the temperature and humidity got, at times reaching what seemed to her almost suffocating levels.

The dock at Mombasa was busy, noisy, and hot as Helen took a deep breath and stepped from the ship's gangway to stand on the African continent for the first time. However, she still had a long way to go before reaching her new home. After clearing immigration and collecting their luggage, Helen and the other missionaries climbed aboard a train headed north to Nairobi, Kenya's capital.

As the train rumbled north, Helen could barely contain herself. She was so excited that she felt like a child as she raced from side to side in the carriage, not wanting to miss one new view of Africa. At each station where the train stopped, she climbed down onto the ground and took in the sights and the smells, the talking and the laughing going on around her.

In Nairobi, the group stayed in a Church Missionary Society guesthouse for several days before resuming their overland journey to Ibambi, Congo. They headed northwest past Lake Victoria and on into Uganda. After crossing Uganda, they came to the edge of Lake Albert, which formed part of the border between Uganda and the Congo. Overnight they caught a steamer across the lake. At 5:30 in the morning Helen sat on the steamer's deck under a mosquito net and caught her first glimpse of the Congo, ablaze in gold, orange, and purple as the sun rose behind the steamer and stretched its rays across the lake and mountains beyond. Helen would never forget the beautiful sight.

When the steamer docked on the other side of Lake Albert, Jack Scholes was waiting for Helen and the others when they disembarked. Jack was the senior WEC missionary in the country, having arrived in the Congo four years before Helen was even born. Helen had met Jack in England when he and his wife, Jessie, were on furlough and had come to stay at WEC headquarters. Helen was delighted to meet up with Jack again. Despite the hot, clammy morning air, Jack's silver, wavy hair was neatly combed.

Although the group had already traveled hundreds

of miles since arriving in Mombasa, Ibambi was still over three hundred miles away over mountains and through the forest.

After clearing Congolese customs and immigration controls, the missionaries and their luggage were loaded into the back of Jack's truck for the journey westward into the Congo. From the edge of Lake Albert, the truck negotiated its way up a series of switchbacks that crept up the mountains skirting the lake. As the truck climbed, Helen caught spectacular panoramas of the mountains and the lake, with Uganda stretching away into the distance on the other side.

The group stopped to sleep and rest at two mission stations along the way, arriving at Ibambi at dusk on March 14, 1953, one month after setting sail from London aboard the *Dunnottar Castle.* Though exhausted, Helen was delighted to have arrived at her new home.

Ibambi looked much like the many villages the missionaries had driven through on their overland trip: palm trees, thatched huts and mud-brick buildings surrounded by banana trees, and chickens pecking at the red earth. The road to the mission house was lined with tall palm trees, beneath which people stood laughing and waving. Helen spotted a homemade sign that read, "Welcome to Ibambi!"

As Helen climbed down from the truck and stretched her legs, Africans crowded around her. They sang choruses and reached out to touch her arms and face, and she blurted out the Swahili sentence she'd memorized for the occasion: "Ninafurahi na furaha kubwa kuwa hapa katikati yenu" (I have great joy to be here among you). The people cheered.

"This is Pastor Ndugu," Jack said, clapping an old man on the back. Pastor Ndugu stepped closer to Helen. The cheering stopped. "We, the church of Jesus Christ in the Congo, and we, her elders, welcome you, our child, into our midst," he said.

Helen was delighted. After qualifying as a doctor and then spending two years training and preparing, she was now a medical missionary and part of a Christian church in the heart of Africa. And how good it felt to her to be called their child.

That night Helen barely slept. She was in the guest room of the Scholeses' home, where she would live while getting accustomed to Africa. It was a simply furnished room with two tea chests, a camp bed, and a folding chair, and it was enough for Helen. All around her she could hear the sounds of monkeys in the trees and the distant howls of other animals.

The next morning Helen was up early as bright sunlight streamed in though the thin cotton curtains. While it was a day for her to rest from the long journey, she was eager to travel to Nebobongo to see firsthand the leprosarium Edith Moules had helped found. However, she learned from Jessie Scholes that several months before, staff from the Belgian Red Cross hospital at nearby Pawa had evacuated Nebobongo's leprosarium and transferred the patients to a newly built, well-equipped leper center at Pawa. Jessie explained that though WEC still operated a maternity center and orphanage in Nebobongo, there wasn't much else to see over there. Most of the old leprosarium and associated village was rapidly being reclaimed by the jungle.

Instead of going to Nebobongo, Helen rested and asked Jessie all manner of questions about life in Ibambi. Jessie told her about the daily routine at the mission compound. Everyone was expected to be up to start the day with a cup of tea at 5:10 a.m. and then be ready for public prayer at the Bible school at 6:30. This was followed by breakfast and private prayer before heading off to work for the day at nine o'clock. The missionaries followed their own schedule throughout the day until dinner at seven o'clock. After dinner a Bible study was held, followed by more prayer and a cup of hot chocolate. All were expected to be in bed by ten o'clock with their hurricane lamps turned off. Excited to be part of the team of dedicated missionaries at Ibambi, Helen enthusiastically followed the routine the next morning.

At around nine o'clock that morning, Jack walked Helen over to the mission office building, where he'd cleared out a room for her to use as a medical clinic. After he left, Helen scanned the room, which had four walls, a tin roof, a concrete floor, a window with shutters but no glass, and a door that opened onto a veranda. She opened the only cupboard in the room and discovered an odd assortment of medicines, from Epsom salts to a bottle of quinine, cough mixture, boric acid to treat cuts, and several bottles of eyedrops. It was a humble beginning, but as Helen studied the room, her imagination soared. *One day,* she told herself, *a grand hospital will stand in this spot, a place where the Congolese people can come for excellent medical care and for spiritual care as well.*

Jack soon returned to Helen's office with a chair, a desk, and a shelf. Helen set to work. She was grateful for the boxes of medical supplies churches in England and Ireland had sent with her, and for the rest of the day she unpacked and organized them. Helen created a simple card system for recording patients' names and details of their treatment. As she placed her tropical medicine textbook on the shelf, she wondered how many times a day she would need to consult it.

That night after work, Helen walked over to the small cemetery where she found C.T. Studd's grave, a simple rectangle of grey concrete on the red clay. Helen stood in silence thinking of all that Norman Grubb and Edith Moules had told her about this great man. She closed her eyes and imagined him walking around Ibambi ministering to people. Afterward she walked quietly back to the Scholeses' house, praying quietly that she would prove worthy to carry on C.T. Studd's mission in the area.

By the next day, word had gotten around the village that the mission's medical clinic was open for business. Old men with walking sticks, mothers carrying babies in their arms, and children with severe skin diseases all arrived at the clinic. For so long Helen had tried to imagine this moment, and now that it was here she felt overwhelmed. She spoke only a few words of Swahili, and she had never actually seen many of the illnesses she'd read about in her tropical disease textbook. She realized it was one thing to pass an exam in Europe but quite another to be confronted with so many sick and needy people standing on the veranda outside her door.

Helen took a deep breath and tried to organize the people who had come to the clinic. Thankfully Jessie came to help her. She divided the patients into lines, one for those with headaches, another for those with coughs, and a third line for those with something else. Helen then set to work examining sick people in batches. With her stethoscope she listened to the chests of those with coughs to determine if they were suffering from tuberculosis (TB) or pneumonia. Those not suffering from either were given a dose of cough medicine. Helen used Jessie as her interpreter to take detailed notes on those who most likely had TB or pneumonia and who would need stronger and more aggressive treatment.

The day sped by in a chaotic whirlwind of faces, illnesses, arguing, and hand waving. Helen suspected some of the people didn't have much wrong with them. They just wanted to see the new woman doctor and the inside of her clinic.

As the week went on, Helen began to feel more confident, even though 150 people a day lined up outside her clinic door for treatment. She also began to pray for a full-time assistant, someone she could train to take responsibility for dispensing medicines.

Sometimes the types of injuries and illnesses

Helen saw defied imagination. The Congo was a dangerous place to live. It seemed that anything and everything could carry disease: the water, food, animal bites, excrement, insects, even the leaves of some trees. Every type of tropical disease flourished in the country as well: yellow fever, black fever, malaria, leprosy. On top of this were the crocodiles in the rivers, deadly snakes in the grass, and leopards in the forest waiting for victims they could attack. Even animals and insects Helen was familiar with did fantastic things. Driver ants traveled in packs of hundreds of thousands and ate their way through things rather than go around them. A sleeping child or adult who did not get out of the way could be eaten alive where he or she lay. The rawness of nature took some getting used to for a person who'd spent her life around sheep and cows.

During her second week running the clinic, Helen spotted a group of men wearing loin cloths coming her way. They carried two poles with a blanket slung between them. As the men got closer, Helen realized there was a man in the blanket. They laid him on the veranda outside the clinic. Helen took one look at the man in the blanket and stepped back. He had a gaping wound in his stomach. Through a series of gestures, Helen learned that someone had thrown a spear at the man's back. The weapon had gone through the man's body, coming out the other side just below his belly button. One man who'd helped carry the wounded patient pantomimed how he'd pulled the rest of the spear out through the front of the patient's body, while another man held the spear out for Helen to examine. It was six feet long and smeared with blood. Helen shuddered. Although she was a doctor, blood and guts still horrified her. She knew she needed to set aside her horror so that she could work out how best to treat the wounded man, who amazingly was still conscious and groaning.

Helen washed her hands and checked the man's pulse and breathing. Both were shallow but steady. Then she felt around the exit wound. Judging from the angle of the wound at which the spear had exited, she thought it could have gone right through his large intestine or nicked his pancreas or liver. If that were the case, it would be too late for the man, since she had neither the equipment to operate on his internal wounds nor anyone to assist her. Helen did her best, cleaning out the entrance and exit wounds with iodine and covering them in a bandage wrapped around the man's torso. Jack brought a camp bed and set it up on the veranda. He placed the wounded man on the bed and covered him with a mosquito net. Helen, Jack, and the men who'd brought the injured man to the clinic settled down around him for the night.

Helen carefully watched the wound for signs of infection, but there seemed to be none. She redressed his wound each day for four days, and on the fifth day the man declared he was better, stood up, and walked away with his friends. Helen was astonished. She didn't know how the spear had managed to go through his body without causing permanent damage. Neither did she know why the wound hadn't become infected. She wrote up her report after the incident that she was certain that she'd see many more patients in the Congo who would defy the odds.

A week later, Helen encountered another life-or-death situation. This time she didn't even have her stethoscope or any iodine with her. Helen had borrowed the Scholeses' car to drive to the nearby market town of Wamba. As she returned home along the road, which skirted the jungle, a group of people flagged her down. "We need help. We need a doctor now. You are Doctor Helen?" one of the men spoke to her in broken French. Helen marveled at how they knew who she was, since they'd never seen each other before.

"Yes," she replied in French. "I am Doctor Helen. But I've been shopping at the market. I don't have my medical bag with me. I have no instruments or medicines with which to help."

"You must come now," the man said. "Our village elder is very sick."

"I wish I could do something," Helen replied, "but I have nothing with which to help your elder. I will go home and get my medical bag and meet you back here as soon as I can. How would that be?"

"No, no! He will be dead soon. You must come now," the man insisted.

Helen gave in. For better or for worse, she was going to follow these strangers into the jungle in an effort to heal a man who was apparently close to death. As she walked, it crossed her mind that she was in a precarious situation. She was alone, no one knew where she was except for the people she was following, and when they got to wherever they were going, she was expected to work some kind of miracle and save their elder's life. But what if he died while she was there? Would they understand that she'd tried her best?

It was damp underfoot as the group trudged through the jungle. Inquisitive monkeys called to each other in the treetops. After walking for about an hour, Helen and the group emerged into a clearing. At one end sat several round huts with thatched roofs. Darkness was falling as they approached the huts, but Helen could see a group of people standing around a fire. On the well-trodden earth beside the fire lay an old man dressed in a loincloth, writhing in pain.

Helen hesitated, then walked over to the man and knelt beside him. She felt his forehead. The old man was burning up. She examined him as best she could by the firelight. He was delirious, and his heart was racing. As Helen examined his legs, it was quickly obvious what was wrong. The man had a fiery-hot abscess the size of a hockey puck in his groin. Instantly, Helen knew that the people were right: this man was dying. And he didn't have long to live unless the enormous amount of pus that had built up under his skin was lanced and the wound cleaned properly. There was no time to get proper medical instruments from the clinic.

Helen looked around. What could she use? Several pygmies had materialized from the bush and were standing on the outskirts of the group by the fire. As always, they carried their iron-tipped arrows. Helen got to her feet, walked to the nearest pygmy, and with a series of gestures asked to borrow his arrow. The pygmy handed it to her, then watched as Helen bent over and ripped off the bottom ten inches of her slip. Holding it up she said in a mixture of broken Swahili and French, "This needs to go into boiling water." Thankfully, one of the men appeared to understand what she was saying. A pot of water near the fire was dragged over, and the water was brought to a boil. Once the water was boiling, the fabric was thrown into it.

Meanwhile, Helen held the tip of the arrow in the fire, watching it turn red-hot. By now everyone in the village had gathered to watch, whispering among themselves and craning their necks to see what was happening. Helen motioned for two of the strongest men to hold the elder down. Then she turned, grasped the arrow from the fire, walked over to the elder, and jabbed the searing end deep into the abscess. A thick stream of gooey, yellow pus gushed up into the air. The crowd gasped while the elder groaned and writhed.

Working quickly, Helen squeezed out as much pus and blood from the abscess as she could and mopped the wound with boiled ribbons of fabric from her slip. Then she used more fabric and wadded up a plug, which she eased into the craterlike hole the lanced abscess had left on the inside of the elder's leg. She bandaged his thigh tight to hold the wad in place.

Before she was finished, Helen could see that the elder's condition had improved. He felt cooler to the touch, and he smiled at her. She had a good feeling. If he could keep the wound clean, the elder had a good chance of getting better. Helen washed her hands, poured boiling water over the arrowhead, and returned it to the astonished pygmy.

Helen gave a few basic instructions to the men on how to care for their patient and promised to return to the side of the road in the morning. If someone was there to guide her back to the village, she would return with medicine to help speed their elder's recovery.

As she trudged back to her car with several escorts from the village, Helen said a silent prayer of thanks. It wasn't often a doctor could save a man's life in such a way without instruments or medicines. Yet the incident sobered Helen. To the locals, she realized she would always be "doctor" before she was anything else. She would have to remember to carry her medical bag with her wherever she went. Feeling the burden of being the only medical missionary doctor within hundreds of miles, she wondered what she could do about it. As young and idealistic as she was, Helen could see that she would be run to the point of exhaustion if she didn't find a way to multiply her impact on the those who inhabited the Congo's jungle.

Chapter 7

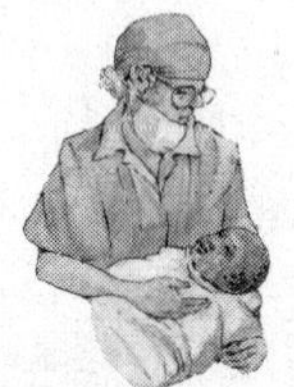

"It's a Thermometer"

A week after the trek into the jungle to save the life of the village elder with the abscess in his groin, paperwork arrived at Ibambi summoning Helen to the Belgian Red Cross hospital at Pawa, fifteen miles north of Ibambi. She was to complete a one-month medical course at the hospital that would license her to officially practice medicine in the Belgian Congo. The Red Cross was responsible for the Belgian government's medical work in the area.

Helen was eager to learn all she could at the Pawa Red Cross hospital. She spent her first two weeks there working under Dr. Kadoner, who'd served with the Belgian colonial medical service for twenty-five years. The doctor gave Helen lots of good advice about practicing medicine in the country. Several other doctors were also stationed at the hospital. One of them, a young leprosy specialist named Dr. Swertz, refused to talk to Helen. Helen wasn't sure whether his decision was because she was young, a female, English, a missionary, or perhaps because of some combination of all these things. Whatever the reason for his refusal to talk to her, Helen found the situation frustrating.

Added to her frustration was the grief Helen felt after receiving a letter from home. For some time, Helen had known that her parents' marriage was not a happy one. It was still a shock to her when she learned that her father had moved out of the family home and was filing for divorce. Somewhere deep down, Helen had always hoped her parents would be able to work out their differences, but now that hope was gone. All she wanted to do was rush home to England and help her mother through her difficult situation, but she realized that being absent during important family events was part of the sacrifice of being a missionary.

At the end of her first week at the Belgian Red Cross hospital, Helen was told that an old man from Ibambi, an active church worker there, had been admitted the day before. When she visited him, she found two of his granddaughters standing glumly beside him. It was obvious the old man was seriously ill. Helen picked up his chart and looked it over. The man had been diagnosed with an internal obstruction for which he needed immediate surgery. In the meantime, he'd been prescribed sulfonamide, an antibiotic, to be taken every four hours.

Two male nurses looked sheepishly at Helen and moved away from the old man's bed when she put down the chart. Helen soon learned why. In Swahili and a little French, she learned from the old man's granddaughters that when the two nurses came on duty in the hospital at six o'clock the night before, they both told the girls their grandfather's condition was serious and that he needed to take sulfonamide pills for it. However, they refused to give him the medication unless he handed over his granddaughters as payment. The old man told the nurses he would rather die than let his granddaughters pay for his treatment in such a way. He urged the two girls to leave him there for the night, which they did. They returned early in the morning to discover their grandfather had been given none of the prescribed pills and his condition had deteriorated.

What Helen heard disgusted and angered her. Nearly all the nurses at the Red Cross hospital were men since most Congolese girls did not have the opportunity to go to school and receive the necessary education to become nurses. *How many girls and women,* Helen wondered, *had male nurses demanded as "payment" for treatment?*

Furious, she searched out Dr. Kadoner. "Some nurses in this hospital are not honorable," she began as she poured out the story the two girls had just told her.

Dr. Kadoner looked bored and, when Helen had finished, simply shrugged his shoulders. "You're not home anymore," he said. "This is Africa. What more can we expect?"

Helen's mouth dropped open at his reply, but no words came out. Was this the best response the doctor could offer? She decided it probably was. Her story had not shaken Dr. Kadoner in the least, as if he knew exactly what was going on in the hospital. In fact, despite her protest, the old man still did not get his pills or the urgent surgery he needed and died the next day.

During the rest of her time at the Red Cross hospital, Helen yearned for a Christian hospital where all patients and their family members would be treated with dignity and respect and where doctors, be they white or black, would hold each other to a high moral standard.

At the end of the one-month medical course at the Red Cross hospital, Helen passed her examination. She was grateful when Dr. Kadoner issued her a license to practice medicine in the Belgian Congo. She was especially grateful when the Scholeses invited her to go with them to a weekend Christian retreat in Poko, 120 miles north. Following her experience at the hospital, Helen decided a strong dose of Christian fellowship was in order. While at the retreat, Helen met another single woman, a widow about her own age. Elizabeth Naganimi knew all the missionaries at Ibambi. After one of the retreat meetings she spoke to Helen. "I feel God has called me to work with you," she said through another missionary who translated Elizabeth's Bangala words into English for Helen.

Refreshed from the fellowship and Bible study she enjoyed at the retreat, Helen returned to Ibambi to continue her work. Elizabeth soon joined her there. Even though she and Helen had only a few words in common, the two got along well. Helen could see that Elizabeth was a fast, intelligent worker, and both women tried hard to learn the other's language so they could communicate and be effective as a team.

Helen and Elizabeth were kept busy with an unending line of patients waiting on the veranda outside the clinic door. Just when Helen thought she'd seen it all, someone would show up with a condition or injury she had not yet encountered. Helen was glad to treat everyone, but deep in her heart she remembered the experience with the old man and his two granddaughters at the Red Cross hospital. Even though she hardly dared admit it to herself, the idea of training Christian medical workers to start their own clinics throughout the Congo took root in her heart. She started praying that if God was in this idea, He would open the way ahead.

One day, about five months after Helen's experience at the Red Cross hospital, a teenage boy came to see her. "What can I do for you?" she asked.

"God has sent me here to see you," the boy replied.

"I'm glad to meet you. What is your name?"

"John Mangadima," the young man replied. "I am a Christian."

"How old are you, John?" Helen asked.

"Sixteen. You are a doctor, right?"

"Yes," Helen responded.

"I want you to teach me how to become a doctor."

Helen stared at John. Becoming a doctor took many years of training, and there was nowhere for a person like him to train in the Belgian Congo.

"I've already studied at the hospital in Pawa for a year and worked as a wound dresser," John said. "I remember you from there."

Helen studied John's face closely but couldn't recall him from among the other young men who worked at the hospital.

Their conversation continued. Helen learned that John was fired from the hospital for speaking up when Dr. Swertz kicked a leper in his presence. She also discovered that John had little education, having never gone past fourth grade because both his parents had leprosy and he had to fend for himself from an early age. As Helen spoke with John, she realized that the chances of his ever becoming a doctor or a nurse were almost zero. Still there was something about him that she was drawn to. Could this sixteen-year-old with a fourth-grade education, who had never been outside the Congo, be the answer to her prayers?

The next day a woman arrived unexpectedly at the clinic. Her face glowed. "I am Mama Damaris," she announced.

"Where are you from?" Helen asked.

"Hell," Mama Damaris replied.

"Who are you?" Helen pressed.

"A woman from hell, but I'm on my way to heaven."

Helen didn't know what to make of Mama Damaris, until John recognized her. "She is the woman I spoke to at the office where I had my labor card stamped yesterday. I told her about Jesus and she believed. Then I told her I was coming here, and she followed me," John said.

Because it seemed to make perfect sense to John and Mama Damaris that she should join them in Ibambi, Helen found her a room in which to stay.

As she prayed that night, Helen didn't know what to think. Was God bringing together an unlikely band of people to form the core of a medical team? She wasn't sure, so she kept praying. And as she prayed, bit by bit it became clear to her that the next step was to start a school to train future nurses. Part of Helen was excited by the prospect, but another part of her was terrified. WEC had a policy of using ministry money only for evangelism, so missionaries who wanted to start an enlarged medical work would have to find a way to pay for it themselves. So far, Helen's friends and supporters in Great Britain had sent enough money and supplies for her to keep the clinic open, but a nursing school was a huge step beyond that. How could she keep one afloat financially?

Despite her doubts and questions, Helen kept an open mind and continued to pray about starting a school. She also contacted supporters back home in England to see if some of them would take on the added challenge of helping finance it. She talked to the leaders of the church and missionaries at Ibambi about her dream. All offered Helen their support in the new venture.

On January 20, 1954, ten months after arriving in the Belgian Congo, Helen opened the nursing school. She had recruited eight teenage boys, including John Mangadima, who was the most educated among them, having worked and studied at the Red Cross hospital. Several of the boys had only four years of primary school education. When Helen gave her first "lecture" at the new school, things didn't go well. "What is this?" she asked the eight boys, holding up a thermometer. Seven of them stared at her blankly.

"It's a thermometer," John replied, using the English word, since there was no word for *thermometer* in Swahili.

"Good," Helen said. "Our thermometers come from England, and they measure a person's body temperature using the Fahrenheit scale. However, here in the Congo we use the European scale, which is Celsius. A healthy person has a temperature of 98.2 degrees Fahrenheit."

As Helen turned to write the number on the blackboard, one of the boys raised his hand and asked, "Excuse me, Doctor. What is the dot between the 8 and the 2 for?"

Helen stopped in her tracks. "That's a decimal point. You do know what a decimal point is, don't you?"

"No, madam," the boy said. Several of the other boys shook their heads along with him.

Helen stood silent. Open in front of her were the only two textbooks she could find on nursing. In a moment of clarity she realized that the boys seated in front of her weren't going to understand much of the material the books contained. Working privately with John, who was intelligent and had gained a lot of experience from his year at the Red Cross hospital, had given Helen a false expectation of what the other boys in the class were capable of learning.

She spent the next several minutes giving the boys a math lesson focusing on decimal points. After she felt that most of them understood, she turned her focus back to the thermometer. To demonstrate its inner workings, she found a small metal ball and a metal ring. She showed the boys how the metal ball was too big to fit through the metal ring. After she heated the metal ring, she showed how the metal ball now fit through it. The boys seemed both amazed and puzzled by this.

Helen explained that when she heated the metal ring it expanded, making the hole in the middle wider and allowing the ball to pass through. She then held up a thermometer and pointed to the mercury in the bowl of the instrument. She explained that mercury was a metal, and when it was heated, like the metal ring, it expanded and squeezed a narrow column of mercury up the thin glass tube inside the thermometer. In fact, she pointed out, the heat from a human body was enough to cause the mercury to expand. If the thermometer was placed under a patient's armpit for a minute or so, after it was removed, one could look at it and read the number at the top of the column of mercury from the scale marked on the side of the thermometer. This number, she said, was equivalent to the person's body temperature.

Although it took a while, the boys began to catch on. Soon they were placing thermometers under each other's arms and reading their body temperatures. It was a small step, but Helen was satisfied with it.

Helen also discovered that an effective way to teach the boys was to have them join her as she treated people who showed up for the clinic each morning. She would point out the symptoms to the boys and then diagnose the patient's medical conditions and the various treatments that could be used. As time went on she would point out the symptoms and then ask the boys to diagnose the condition. At first they mostly got it wrong, but gradually they began to match symptoms to illnesses.

Helen taught the boys how to use a stethoscope to listen to a patient's heart and lungs. One day, after listening to a patient's lungs, she announced to the boys, "This patient has pneumonia. How do I know that?"

None of the boys could answer the question. Helen gave her stethoscope to John and told him to use it to listen to the woman's lungs while she breathed.

"I can hear a deep, raspy rhythmic sound," John said after listening to the patient's breathing.

"Very good," Helen said. "Now put the end of the stethoscope against your chest and listen to your breath." She waited as John did as instructed. "Can you hear a difference?"

"Yes," John replied.

"Now put the stethoscope against Yokana's chest and listen." Yokana was one of the other students in the nursing class. "What does it sound like?" Helen asked.

"It sounds like my chest did," John replied.

"You are right," Helen said. "You and Yokana do not have pneumonia, so you both have normal breathing sounds. But this woman has pneumonia, and that is why her chest sounded the way it did when she breathed. That is the sound of pneumonia. Remember it and remember the sound of your own healthy chest. The next time you hear that deep, raspy sound you will know your patient probably has pneumonia."

The other boys all took turns listening to the patient's chest and then to their own, noting the difference. As time went on, by listening with a stethoscope they began to recognize those patients who showed up at the clinic suffering from pneumonia.

Helen found teaching the boys to be challenging work, and she knew the course was difficult for them. Within weeks, three of them dropped out, unwilling to discipline themselves to study. But with Helen's guidance, the other five worked hard.

When Helen described to the village church her vision for setting up a small hospital in Ibambi, the leaders and congregation got behind the endeavor.

Helen had already received permission to build the small hospital in front of the clinic. The church took on responsibility for building the new structure, which would consist of two wards. One would have twenty-four beds for women and children, while the other had eight beds for men. The building would contain a large hall for medical consultations and individual rooms for maternity patients, people needing surgery, and those with contagious diseases. During part of their day, the boys training to become nurses worked alongside church members, first making the necessary mud bricks and then using them to build the walls. Once the bricks had been made and the walls built, the boys worked with a group of local evangelists to weave and put in place thick matting for the roof.

Construction took nine months, and in September 1954, the two wards were completed and officially opened with a dedication service. Now the five boys could concentrate fully on their nursing studies while Helen could admit patients who needed to be hospitalized rather than send them to the Belgian Red Cross hospital in Pawa.

Slowly, painstakingly, Helen wrote a new curriculum tailored to the boys' needs. Each night after class she typed out pages from the two Red Cross textbooks. To make the material easier to study and understand, she added her own information and ideas.

Much to Helen's delight, the five boys who stayed with the nurse training program studied hard and overcame their natural shyness around white people while learning to ask Helen many questions.

It took close to two years, but on October 25, 1955, all five boys were ready to sit their nursing certificate exams. Helen drove them to the Red Cross hospital in Pawa, and hardly a word was said all the way there. Helen knew that the boys were anxious. Sitting an exam was a big step, especially for those who hadn't even finished primary school.

In Pawa, twelve Red Cross students joined them in a waiting room at the back of the laboratory building. Inside, a government doctor was ready to ask each student individually the questions on the exam. Everyone spoke in French except the boys from Ibambi. Helen could sense their confidence melting away over their lack of French, which showed that they were uneducated boys from the jungle. Helen was asked to sit in on the oral exams and help with translation if necessary. She sat tensely, hardly daring to look at her boys lest she show how anxious she was.

One by one all seventeen boys taking the exam were asked medical questions. The students from the Red Cross hospital could parrot back answers to standard nursing questions, but when asked what they would do in specific situations, most of them failed in their responses. The boys from Ibambi, on the other hand, grew more confident when they were asked questions that showed they had to think for themselves. Helen knew this was because of all the times she had drilled them as they followed her around tending to patients.

As soon as the exam was over, the points were tallied and each student's score written on the blackboard. Yokana from the Ibambi group scored the highest marks of all seventeen students with 95 percent. John Mangadima scored third with 85 percent. Two of the other three boys from Ibambi received passing grades, and only one of them came up short.

With the exam over, everyone whooped for joy. All their hard work had paid off. Four jungle boys from Ibambi were now registered nursing assistants, and the one who did not pass was confident that he would pass the next year. Helen was delighted. She couldn't imagine anything on the horizon that would take away her joy.

Chapter 8

Mama Luka

"What?!" Helen felt her voice raise to a pitch, but she didn't care. "It's not right." She put her hands on her hips and added, "I won't do it. The mission board can't make me. And next week! Do they think I can pack up everything and be gone in a week?"

Jack Scholes stood in the clinic looking uncomfortable. "I know it won't be easy," he said, "but they're sure this is the right thing to do. You can make a great hospital at Nebobongo."

Helen was so angry she spit out her words. "I've already started a hospital here in Ibambi! This is where God laid it on my heart to start. Just yesterday, four of our boys passed their nursing aid exams. That's a huge milestone no one but me seems to want to celebrate. They're ready to man the hospital here—at Ibambi—here where the patients come, where our clinic and dispensary are located. Why would the committee want to change that? There is plenty of room for us to grow here."

"I don't know all their thinking, Helen," Jack said soothingly, "but they feel it would be best for everyone."

"But it's not best for me. It's ridiculous!" Helen retorted. "I want to speak to the board."

"It will just start an argument. Their minds seem set."

"I don't care," Helen snapped. "This is my clinic, my dream, and I have a right to defend it."

"If you must," Jack said. "I'll ask the members to make time for you at seven tonight."

For the rest of the day, Helen seethed. How dare the mission board tell her she needed to move? Surely they were aware of the amount of money and work she'd already put into the clinic and the plans she had for the hospital. Besides, she didn't know any of the people at the local church in Nebobongo, and she didn't want to.

By evening Helen was in quite a state. She'd gone over in her head every argument she could think of and was ready for battle with the mission board. At seven o'clock she checked her watch and walked toward the door of the room where the meeting was to be held. "Helen, shall we pray together before you go in?" Helen heard Jessie behind her.

Helen swung around. "Pray!" she burst out. "No, not now."

Jessie looked at Helen and then got down on her knees. "Lord, we bring this situation to You," she said, "Please help Helen find grace and peace at this time. May Your will be done here tonight, not our own."

Helen snorted.

"You know there are two sides to this, Helen," Jessie said, getting up from her knees. "The mission board isn't trying to hurt you. They're trying to look ahead. I believe they want Ibambi to be seen as a place to come to study the Bible and learn, and they think a Christian hospital here will overshadow that. Someone here would have to be responsible to feed everyone who came to the hospital, and in the end, we'd have to have a small village to house the relatives of patients. To keep it all going would be a tremendous commitment from a lot of people. At Nebobongo they are better set up for a hospital like yours."

Helen didn't say a word. She just listened to Jessie. Slowly she began to wonder if she was being unreasonable. Perhaps, as Jessie said, there was another side to the matter. But if she moved to Nebobongo, Helen knew that the responsibility for everything from raising money for salaries to checking the water supply for mosquitoes would fall on her.

The door to the room opened. "Sorry to keep you waiting," Jack said. "Please, come in."

As Helen walked into the room and sat down, she was at peace. She listened respectfully as members of the mission board outlined their views as to why she should move to Nebobongo. Somehow it didn't matter so much to her anymore. She thought of the Bible verse that said, "All things work together for good to them that love God, to them who are the called according to his purpose" (Romans 8:28).

There was no argument, no bitter debate after all. At the end of the meeting Helen agreed to follow the mission board's recommendation. On October 30, 1955, she drove out of Ibambi behind the mission's truck. She was on her way from the local church in Ibambi to Nebobongo with Elizabeth Naganimi, the four boys who'd just earned their nursing certificates, the one student who narrowly missed out, Mama Damaris, and Agoya, his wife, Taadi, and their six children.

As the convoy made its way north, Helen prayed that she would be equal to the task ahead of her. An English couple, the Colemans, had been leading the work in Nebobongo but had gone home on furlough. This meant that the only other qualified medical person there was Florence Stebbing—or Stebby, as everyone called her. Stebby was a nurse and midwife who maintained a small maternity unit in the village. Besides the maternity unit, two other mission buildings were at Nebobongo. They housed thirty-eight children left behind when their parents suffering from leprosy were transferred from the leprosarium to the Belgian Red Cross hospital in Pawa. Five local Christian women lived with and cared for the children. This was a lot for Helen to inherit, and even more when you factored in the 150 or more people who would follow Helen and her nurses daily to Nebobongo for medical treatment.

The day after her arrival, Helen went to work accompanied by those who had moved with her from Ibambi, along with some local church leaders. Together they walked the full length and breadth of the property. Helen was amazed at how quickly the jungle had reclaimed what had been the leprosarium and the housing that went along with it. The buildings were so overgrown they were barely visible, and in some cases trees grew out from inside of them. There would be no reusing these buildings, though Helen hoped to recover some of the wood from them.

By the end of the day, Helen had a clear vision. A new village for the workers needed to be built on the hill to the west, new water holes bored, toilets installed, vegetable gardens established, and a kiln set up to produce the thousands of mud bricks needed to build the new hospital.

At the same time that Helen and the workers began construction, Helen became concerned for the education of the children in the orphanage. She put out a call for a teacher, but when no one came forward, she set aside three hours of her time each morning to teach them. To her, these children were part of the generation that would rise up to become future nurses, doctors, and teachers in the Congo. Someone had to ensure that these boys and girls got a good start with their reading and writing. Besides teaching the children and helping with the hospital construction, Helen still held daily medical clinics and helped Stebby in the maternity unit. One of Helen's first surgeries at Nebobongo was an emergency cesarean section to save a pygmy woman who had been unable to deliver her baby in the jungle. It was Helen's first time performing a cesarean section. During her time in medical school, she had done her best to avoid doing surgery. Despite her best efforts, the baby was stillborn. To make matters worse, the mother contracted an infection after the surgery and died ten days later. It was a bitter blow for Helen, who grieved the death of any patient under her care.

The days at Nebobongo turned into weeks, and then months. The rainy season deluged the place, and hurricane-strength winds whipped the roof off the clinic pavilion, blowing it into the jungle. The road in and out of the village was so deep in mud that in some places trucks had to lay down planks to drive across. Despite the weather, acres of crops, including rice, peanuts, manioc, pineapples, paw paws, and plantains, were planted around the village.

Through it all, Helen wrote hundreds of personal letters and a fortnightly newsletter to those back home in Great Britain, updating them on her progress and the needs in Nebobongo. Helen followed what she called the Müller Method of fundraising, named after George Müller, who had cared for thousands of orphans in England. The method entailed praying about a project and then waiting for 10 percent of the money needed to launch the project to come in. At that point Helen would begin and continue to pray that the rest of the money for the project would arrive. Following this method, bit by bit the medical compound began to emerge from the jungle.

By the end of her first year at Nebobongo, Helen and her team had accomplished a great deal. The maternity unit had been improved and was delivering about forty babies a month. Stebby and Helen were also training twelve women, including Mama Damaris, to become registered midwives; and two new brick hospital wards were up and running, housing fifty patients. Helen had also won the love and admiration of the local Congolese in and around Nebobongo. They'd taken to referring to her with the endearing term "Mama Luka," after Luke, also a physician and the writer of both the New Testament Gospel bearing his name and the Book of Acts. Helen was touched by their love and trust.

Helen suspected that the mission board in Ibambi had sent her off to Nebobongo knowing they were giving her an impossible task. However, with God's help she had found the reserves of energy and strength needed to keep going and stay focused. Now the hospital, clinic, orphanage, and medical training program were growing fast, too fast, in fact. Helen felt she needed another doctor to come alongside so she could branch out and move on to the next phase of her vision—setting up forty-eight small medical clinics stretching out in a figure-eight pattern around Nebobongo. These clinics would be manned by workers she was training. Every two weeks she would bring more medicine and equipment to the clinics, examine the difficult patients, and perform minor surgeries. Helen felt this was the most efficient way to get medical help to people who were scattered throughout the jungle around Nebobongo.

In early 1957, the WEC missionary board agreed with Helen regarding the need for another doctor and sent a young British surgeon, Dr. John Harris, and his wife, Elsie, to help Helen. The Harrises had been working farther north in the Belgian Congo when they agreed to relocate. At first Helen was delighted to have the Harrises working with her, but she soon learned what the word *help* meant to John Harris. The doctor was a trained surgeon, whereas Helen's specialized training was in treating tropical diseases. This ranked Dr. Harris higher up on the medical qualifications tier. Although Helen understood that, the doctor was also a man. While it had been perfectly fine for Helen to be in charge at Nebobongo, now that a highly qualified, white male doctor was living there, she was expected to surrender leadership to him. From the moment he arrived, Dr. Harris had taken control of the hospital, the clinics, teaching the nursing students, and even running the morning Bible study.

Helen fought hard not to give in to bitterness as she saw all of her hard work taken in another direction under Dr. Harris, who had a different style of leadership. While Helen felt that everyone who worked with her belonged to one big family, Dr. Harris viewed the medical workers and staff functioning as a well-oiled machine, with each person having his or her specific task. Helen tried to explain to him the way she'd raised money for the various buildings and how she had managed to keep everything going. Instead of thanking her for this herculean task, Dr. Harris shook his head in disapproval. "From now on, all moneys will be collected before a new project begins. It's the sensible way to go about things," he told Helen, despite the fact that what he considered to be "unsensible" had actually been quite successful.

John Harris also had a different vision for the Nebobongo medical compound. Perhaps because he was a surgeon, he wanted to develop the wards into a fine surgical hospital. As far as Helen could see, this would always require white people running it. She tried to conceal her sadness as she set up the first of the forty-eight medical clinics. Helen now spoke fluent Swahili, which helped her as she traveled from village to village, laying out her plan.

The plan was straightforward. Helen explained to village elders that she wanted them to provide her with a clinic consisting of a one-room house surrounded by a large veranda. The room would contain a bed, a desk, a chair, cooking utensils, and a cupboard. Once the village made the building available, Helen would send a nurse to man the clinic or, if a nurse was not available, train a local Christian to do so. Helen would be responsible for stocking the clinic with drugs such as quinine, Epsom salts, kaolin, boracic powder, and aspirin. She would even provide a concoction she'd formulated to treat hookworm and roundworm. She would also provide tongue depressors, cotton swabs, and medical equipment such as stethoscopes, otoscopes, and microscopes. Helen herself would visit each clinic once a month to diagnose difficult cases, perform minor surgeries, talk to people in the village about hygiene and other health issues, and pray with and encourage clinic staff.

Before long, Helen had all forty-eight clinics up and running. They soon had an impact on the general health of the area. Helen spent the first two weeks of each month traveling from clinic to clinic, six per day. Some of the villages lay along tracks that her truck could barely maneuver. When it rained, Helen was left to plow through mud and flooded roads. Sometimes she got stuck and the locals would rescue her and her vehicle. At other times, the truck would break down, requiring Helen to crawl underneath it or lean over the engine to diagnose the problem. It could be any number of things, including dirty spark plugs, a clogged carburetor, a burst hose, pitted points, or a broken axle or exhaust pipe. After fixing the problem, Helen would crank the truck back to life and head on her way. When she arrived at a clinic, usually five hundred, sometimes a thousand people were there to greet her. Not all of them came for medical attention. Helen's reputation as the unstoppable Mama Luka had gone before her—she could do more to heal a sick child or baby than all the witch doctors in the area combined. People wanted to see her, shake her hand, and look her in the eyes. Helen took it all in stride. This was the work God had called her to pioneer, and that belief energized her. In her "spare time," Helen put together a medical textbook in Swahili. It was a labor of love as she collected all of the material, drew diagrams, and typed endless drafts of the book.

By the beginning of 1958, the constant strain of so much travel keeping the clinics stocked and running took its toll. Helen became sick with amebic dysentery and couldn't seem to get better. She was weary and worried about the future of the Belgian Congo. Like other African countries colonized by European powers, the Congo wanted its independence and to regain control of its people and resources. In late 1955, political leaders in Belgium had announced that they would work to make the Congo an independent country within thirty years. This caused an uproar in the Congo's bigger towns, and Helen could sympathize with the local people. It seemed to her that every other week African countries across the continent, such as Libya, Sudan, and Ghana, were gaining their independence. It seemed impossible to imagine the Congolese waiting patiently for another thirty years to receive theirs.

In mid-1958, Helen applied to WEC to go home to England on furlough. Although she called it a furlough, she had serious doubts about whether she would return to the Congo. She felt that she'd already accomplished much during her service in the country, and that people were alive and enjoying better health care because of the clinics she had pioneered and devoted herself to. Yet she still felt an underlying frustration at having to relinquish her leadership role and make her vision for ministry subservient to that of men.

Helen received permission to head home on furlough. On the way back to England, she decided to visit her father, who had moved from England to the British protectorate of Nyasaland in south central Africa. Her father had invited her to visit, informing Helen that by the time she arrived, he would be married again, and she would be able to meet her stepmother. Helen's parents' divorce had been granted several months before.

With the arrangements made, Helen said good-bye, left Nebobongo, and traveled over 400 miles south to the head of Lake Tanganyika, where she caught a boat that took her 420 miles south to the foot of the lake. Her father was waiting for her when she stepped off the boat. Helen was glad to see him and was soon introduced to his new wife, Margaret. The couple had been married in Nyasaland the previous week. Martin explained that Margaret Montgomery had been employed as a school inspector in Wales, where he had met her. Before leaving Great Britain, he'd traveled to Wales to say good-bye to many of his old friends. But instead of saying good-bye, Helen's father had discovered that he had a lot in common with Margaret. The couple wrote to each other after Martin left for Africa, and after a while Margaret had agreed to come to Africa and marry him.

From Mpulungu at the foot of Lake Tanganyika, Helen climbed into the car with her father and stepmother and set off for Nyasaland. After two days driving, they arrived at Mzuzu, Nyasaland, where Helen's father was the principal of a new secondary school.

During the next five days Helen saw the sights of northern Nyasaland, visited the shore of Lake Malawi, and caught up on family news. The Roseveare family now comprised four members, including Helen, who were living in Africa. Her father's brother Edward was an Anglican priest in Cape Town, South Africa, and his other brother, Richard, was the Anglican bishop of Accra in Ghana. Helen's brother, Bob, and wife, Ione, and their children still lived in Natal, South Africa, though they were presently back in England visiting friends and family. Helen looked forward to catching up with Bob there.

After five days together in Mzuzu, the family loaded Helen's father's car once more and set out on a 750-mile drive to Nairobi. Helen was glad to just be able to sit for a while. Even though she'd enjoyed sightseeing with her energetic father and stepmother, she still felt weak from her bout of amebic dysentery, and just sitting while her father drove was like a tonic to her. Five days later, Helen bid farewell to her father and stepmother and went to stay for two days with a friend, who would get her to the airport in Nairobi to catch her flight for the final leg of her journey back to England.

Chapter 9

Independence

The first thing Helen did upon arrival back in England was visit her mother in her new home in Bromley in Southeast London. It was bittersweet to see her again. Her mother had aged and had developed rheumatoid arthritis, making it difficult for her to do things around the house. Helen helped where she could, but she wasn't feeling well herself. After struggling for a month at home, she visited a doctor for a full medical checkup. The next day she was admitted to the hospital, still suffering from the amebic dysentery she'd developed in the Congo. She was treated for two weeks in the hospital before being well enough to leave.

While she lay in her hospital bed, Helen planned a tour of churches and visits with various groups across the United Kingdom that had supported her work in the Congo. She also tuned in to the BBC to listen for any news updates on what was happening in the Belgian Congo. It seemed the Congolese people were determined to have their independence sooner rather than later. As she listened to BBC radio and read articles in local newspapers, Helen agonized over whether to return to the Congo. In some ways she felt defeated. Yes, she'd done some good in the Congo, but there was still so much more that needed to be done. Helen even wondered if it would be easier to do what she felt called to do if she were a married woman. Surely male doctors would respect her more if she had a husband to back her up. After getting out of the hospital, Helen bought the latest fashion clothes and had her hair permed in a modern style in preparation for her speaking and follow-up tour of Great Britain. She had hopes of finding a man to marry! Despite her effort to look fashionable and attract a husband, she did not find one.

Helen prayed that God would show her what to do next, but nothing clear came to her. She decided to further her medical knowledge by taking a job as a locum (temporary fill-in doctor) first at Mildmay Hospital in London and then at Newport Hospital in Wales. She worked hard at both hospitals and enjoyed many aspects of her work. Everyone spoke English, which took the strain out of communicating with people. The supply cupboards were stocked with clean linens and towels, and when they were taken from the cupboard, more would appear to replace them from the huge modern electric laundry in the hospital basement. Helen thought back to Nebobongo, where the nurses had to wash all the hospital linens by hand and hang them on tree branches to dry and bleach in the sun. And the medicines—antibiotics, painkillers, anesthetics—how many times had she done her best without these items in the Congo?

Being free of the constant strain to raise finances was also a respite for Helen. For the first time in her life, she was receiving a regular paycheck. Week after week she was able to put money into her bank account. She sent much of what she saved back to the Congo to keep the clinics running, but this money was being replenished with each new paycheck, and she still had money left over to help her mother.

As 1959 progressed, the political situation in the Belgian Congo heated up. On November 1 that year, Helen opened the *Guardian* newspaper to read:

> Stanleyville: Security police today arrested M Patrice Lumumba, president of the Congolese National Movement (MNC), after two days of rioting which is reported to have resulted in the deaths of more than 70 people.
>
> Military law is in force in Stanleyville: gatherings of more than five people are banned, a curfew has been imposed between 6:00 p.m. and 5:00 a.m. and all bars and places of entertainment have been closed. At the African Hospital, four teams of five doctors each are

> working shifts to treat the scores of injured who are being brought in hourly.

Helen could only imagine the conditions the doctors were working under.

Soon after his capture, Lumumba was put on trial and sentenced to sixty-nine months in prison for encouraging the Congolese people to practice civil disobedience, which the Belgian government said had led to the riots. A short time later, Helen read that Lumumba had been released from jail to attend the Congolese Round Table Conference to be held in Brussels, Belgium, in mid-January 1960. The purpose of the conference was to finalize the future of the Congo as an independent country.

By now, Helen had been home in Great Britain for a year and a half and knew she needed to make a decision: would she return to a very unpredictable future in the Congo or stay in England and make a life for herself there?

As Helen prayed, she felt a quiet reassurance settle over her that she was supposed to return to Nebobongo and continue her work as a medical missionary. On May 22, 1960, Helen boarded a Castle Line ship bound for Mombasa, Kenya. Traveling with her were two new WEC missionary recruits, twenty-four-year-old Bill McChesney from the United States and Elaine de Rusett, an Australian nurse with midwifery training, both also headed to Nebobongo. Bill and Elaine had just completed their French language study in Belgium. During the three-and-a-half-week voyage,

Helen tutored them in Swahili. At each port of call, the three of them would listen for news updates as to what was happening in the Belgian Congo. Following the Round Table Conference in Brussels, Independence Day in the Congo was set for June 30, 1960. The trio of missionaries would arrive exactly two weeks before that date.

Upon arrival in Mombasa, Helen, Bill, and Elaine prepared for the fifteen-hundred-mile overland trip to Nebobongo. Kenyan immigration officials didn't want to let the three of them off the ship. "You know the Congo is becoming independent in two weeks, don't you?" an immigration officer asked Helen in English.

"Yes, we are aware of that," she replied.

"Kenya already has a wave of white refugees fleeing the Congo. There are more coming every day. We cannot be responsible for any more. I suggest you stay on the ship and complete the voyage back to England," the immigration officer added.

Helen shook her head. "I'm a medical doctor, and she is a nurse," she said, pointing to Elaine. "We have a hospital and many medical clinics to run. And that will be just as important after independence as before, don't you think?"

The immigration officer muttered under his breath. "Well, if you insist. But before I stamp your passport I need proof that each of you can pay to get yourselves out of the Congo and back onto a ship if things don't go well. We cannot take in every white person who flees."

As she took out a copy of her bank statement and showed it to the immigration officer, Helen was glad she'd saved some of her earnings in case something like this happened.

Soon the trio were on their way. On the train ride to Nairobi, Helen watched Bill and Elaine's excitement as they moved from side to side in the carriage to take in the sights of Africa through the train windows. She smiled as she recalled how she'd done the same thing seven years before. Now, to her, it was good to be back in Africa. It felt like home.

The trip retraced the route Helen had taken years before. When they reached Ibambi the missionaries enjoyed an enthusiastic welcome. As Helen had been initially, Bill was stationed at Ibambi, where he would repair and maintain WEC vehicles. After spending the night in Ibambi, Helen and Elaine traveled on to Nebobongo the next morning. Back in Nebobongo, an enthusiastic crowd of several hundred thronged to welcome back Mama Luka. They had even learned a new hymn to perform for her as she arrived.

In Nebobongo, Helen found John and Elsie Harris weary and glad to hand over the hospital work to Helen as they left on furlough. Settling into the life of the village once more, Helen was glad to have Elaine working with her. Elaine's can-do Australian attitude blended well with her pioneering spirit.

While Helen found many things were the same as before she left on furlough, some things in the village were different. With independence just days away, everyone wondered if violence and turmoil would erupt in the country. Would the Congolese accept white people overseeing them anymore? Helen wasn't about to blame them if they did not want to. Belgian colonists living in the country controlled 95 percent of the Congo's wealth and resources, over which the locals would surely want greater control. Then there was the question of how the Congolese would manage the affairs of such a large and diverse country with a population of nearly seventeen million people who spoke over two hundred different tribal languages. Unlike the situation in many other African colonies, the Belgians had not prepared the native population for independence. In the entire country, only seventeen Congolese men had ever graduated from university, and the Belgian government had actively discouraged the Congolese from studying abroad. Along with other missionaries in the area, Helen prayed that somehow things would work out in the country.

Helen's first brush with Congolese self-government came on the eve of Independence Day. Helen, along with the three other white nurses at Nebobongo, Elaine de Rusett, Florence Stebbing, and Winnie Davies, were summoned to a meeting of the local Christian elders and the male nurses from the hospital. The meeting had just started when Helen arrived, but as she walked into the room she sensed those running it had an important announcement to make. A few minutes later, Joseph Bumukumu, a village elder, cleared his throat and raised his voice so that everyone could hear, saying, "We want to appoint an African to lead the hospital. It's happening everywhere. At the Red Cross in Pawa, Dr. Kadoner has handed authority for the hospital over to Gwo-gwo."

Helen took a deep breath at this. Gwo-gwo was a hard worker, but he was only an orderly. How could he possibly run a hospital?

Joseph continued. "We want John Mangadima to be our new hospital director."

Silence fell over the room as Helen prayed for wisdom in how to react. The silence was broken when John stood to address the meeting. "Brothers," he began, "I can be in charge of the nurses and even the general administration, if that's what you want. But we cannot function without our doctors, and I could not be over them. They are far more knowledgeable than I am."

The local men nodded, and Helen smiled. Everyone seemed satisfied. John had been nominated to be hospital director and had nominated Helen to continue in the role. Now it was a white woman managing the hospital at the invitation of the local Congolese. Everyone breathed a sigh of relief.

That night, as Helen lay in bed, she thought about what had happened. Surely similar scenarios must be occurring all over the Congo right now. There was not a single Congolese doctor in the country, nor had there ever been one as far as she knew, and yet many hospitals and clinics were about to be taken over by local nurses. Helen was grateful that the Christians in Nebobongo could work across racial divides to provide the best medical care possible for their people.

As she drifted off to sleep, Helen wondered how the events of the following morning, Thursday, June 30, 1960—Congolese Independence Day—might play out. No one seemed to know exactly what would happen. Would the newspapers still be printed? Would the radio station stay on the air or trains continue to crisscross the country? It all depended on how thousands of white colonials, mainly Belgians, chose to hand over their areas of expertise.

The next day a new nation, the Republic of the Congo, was born. Executive power in the new government was now shared between a president and a prime minister. Joseph Kasa-Vubu became the first democratically elected president of the country, and Patrice Lumumba the first prime minister.

In Nebobongo everything went well on Independence Day. The day began with a morning prayer service followed by a football match against a neighboring village. The local people beamed with pride, and random cries of "Uhuru!" (freedom) were heard throughout the day. A delegation of elders visited Helen at the hospital. They wore woven hats and garlands of flowers. Helen stepped out onto the veranda to greet them. The other white medical staff joined Helen there as Mayaribu, the village chief, offered her a bouquet of flowers and a basket of eggs. "We are glad you have remained with us," he said, "and we invite you to stay with us now that we have independence."

Helen wiped tears from her eyes as she accepted the gifts. *Perhaps Congolese independence would go smoothly after all,* she thought.

A week later, the Belgian commander of the Congo Forces called the native Congolese military together at Leopoldville, the country's capital, and informed them that despite independence, nothing had changed for them. There would be no promotions, no change of command. Everything would be exactly as it was before independence. Within days of learning that the Belgians intended to maintain military control in the country, Congolese garrisons throughout the land mutinied, which led to rioting in the streets.

In response to the crisis, Prime Minister Lumumba fired the Belgian commander and replaced him with a Congolese sergeant major. Despite this, the rioting continued. Much of the rioters' anger was aimed at any white person they could find. Helen began hearing reports that white-owned properties were being looted and burned and white people assaulted.

On Thursday, July 15, 1960, the situation in the country reached the point where the missionaries serving in and around Ibambi had to decide what they would do. They had heard reports that ten thousand Belgian colonials were fleeing the country by bus, car, or train or on foot. It was hard to get precise news of what was happening. From what she heard, Helen gathered that Moise Tshombe, leader of Conféderation des Associations Tribales du Katanga, or CONAKAT, had declared the southern province of Katanga, which was rich in minerals, to be a separate independent country. Tshombe favored continued ties with Belgium and asked the Belgian government to send military officers to recruit and train a Katangese army.

Tensions ran high as the gathered missionaries discussed the unstable and fluid situation that now existed. Some missionaries wanted to stay, while others thought the women and children should be sent to safety until things settled down. In the end it was decided that the missionaries should each pray about their situation and then do what they felt was best for them and their families.

Helen felt no hesitation. As far as she was concerned, she'd come to help the local people, and she would stay with them. Fifteen missionaries and their families serving around the region, including Florence Stebbing, decided to drive fifty miles north to Paulis, where they would be evacuated by airplane and flown to safety.

Once everyone who gathered at Ibambi had made his or her decision, and after a round of goodbyes, Helen returned to Nebobongo. Once there she locked the door to her house behind her. As she went to bed, Helen began wondering if she'd done the right thing. It was a very dark night, and as it dragged on, Helen could sense the voice of fear growing inside her, whispering scary and unsettling things in her head, until the sound of a rat scurrying across her roof left her trembling uncontrollably. She looked at the clock. It was 2:00 a.m. Helen realized she couldn't go on living with this level of fear. She needed to be reassured that her life was firmly in God's hands. She slipped out of bed and onto her knees, asking God to free her from the fear that had crept into her thoughts. Then she prayed for someone to come and be with her to keep her company. Within seconds she heard a knock. Helen's heart raced as she answered the door. Standing outside were Mama Taadi and Mama Damaris.

"What has happened?" Helen asked.

"I have come to keep you company, Mama Luka," Mama Taadi said. "God woke me up and told me to come here now."

Mama Damaris's eyebrows raised in surprise. "That's what happened to me too. I was praying just now, and God told me to get out of bed and come to your house."

Helen hugged both women and welcomed them inside. It was good to have friends to be with, and it was even better to know that God was watching over her and answering her prayers.

In the morning, Helen heard another knock at her door. This time it was two veteran missionaries from Egbita, twenty-five miles to the northwest. Agnes Chansler and Margery Cheverton each carried a suitcase. "We have closed our mission station for now," Margery informed Helen. "When we were praying last night, God told us we should come here to support your work. Do you have room for us?"

Helen nodded, unable to speak.

"Well, good then," Agnes replied. "We'll settle in and start work this afternoon. I was thinking I might take the load of the children's work off you, and Margery is great with administration."

Once again Helen thanked God for confirming her decision to stay put at Nebobongo.

Over the next few weeks, Helen and her team faced many challenges. The Belgian government ordered all of its civil servants to leave the country, and Dr. Swertz from the Red Cross hospital at Pawa left with them. This put Helen as the only medical doctor within a two-hundred-mile radius. Supplies of drugs dwindled, and Helen had to refuse treatment to adults to save what drugs she had on hand for critically ill children. The outlook seemed grim. On the radio Helen heard a United Nations organization spokesman announce that no qualified teachers were left in the country and to train up enough Congolese teachers would take at least five years. Food supplies were beginning to dwindle, and many native people rose up to challenge those white people who had stayed.

Although an independent missionary doctor, Helen was ordered by the government to become a visiting doctor at the Wamba hospital, twenty-five miles south, for two days a week. Helen was also given the job of carrying out medical inspections of the nearby prison in Wamba. Neither job went well. Like the hospital in Nebobongo, the hospital at Wamba suffered from a severe shortage of drugs and medical supplies. And at the prison Helen would find twelve prisoners locked up together in a cell measuring nine by twelve feet. The prisoners had no toilet facilities, and the filth and stench inside the jail were overwhelming. Most of the prisoners were suffering from dysentery and malaria, and Helen administered pills to the inmates, though given their condition she knew they wouldn't do much good.

Overwhelmed by the conditions the inmates were forced to endure, Helen approached the prison commandant as to why those under his care must endure such harsh conditions.

"Because it's a prison," the commandant answered, unmoved.

"But men are dying in there every day," Helen retorted.

The commandant shrugged. "They are criminals, and this is prison," was his reply.

Helen knew there was no point in pursuing the matter.

Meanwhile, unrest in the Congo continued. The Belgian government seemed to have no intention of giving up control of lucrative mineral rights in the country. It sent six thousand troops to the Congo to protect those white people still running the mining industries. Internal fighting in the country only grew worse. Prime Minister Lumumba appealed to both the United Nations and the United States to send soldiers to replace the Belgian troops who were not welcome in the new republic. He wanted them to overthrow the new independent government of the province of Katanga, putting the area back under the control of the Republic of the Congo. The United States refused to become involved, though UN troops did arrive, but for the sole purpose of keeping the peace and not to deal with the situation in Katanga.

The Republic of the Congo descended further into chaos. In desperation the prime minister turned to the Soviet Union, asking for help with restoring peace and political order.

Suddenly, the Republic of the Congo became the center of an international conflict between the United Nations, the United States, and the Soviet Union. No one knew what would happen next.

Chapter 10

A Dark Evil

As 1961 arrived, Helen felt sure it was going to be just as challenging as the previous year. Given the political uncertainty and spiraling violence in their country, many Congolese were taking out their frustrations on white people who remained in the Congo. Some of the worst offenders, Helen learned, were men and boys.

The closing months of 1960 had brought high political drama to the country. After Prime Minister Lumumba requested help from the Soviet Union to put down the rebellion in Katanga province, Soviet aid and military advisors began arriving in the Congo. That in turn led to a showdown between the Congo's prime minister and president. President Kasa-Vubu publicly denounced Lumumba and dismissed him as prime minister. Lumumba pushed back, and a political stalemate developed between president and prime minister. To break the standoff, on September 14, 1960, Colonel Joseph Mobutu, the Congolese army chief of staff, led a coup d'état and overthrew the elected government. The next day Lumumba was put under house arrest at the prime minister's residence.

With the prime minister under arrest, the Soviet Union demanded his immediate release, as did the secretary-general of the United Nations. At the same time, the United States offered assistance through the CIA to the new government that came to power after the coup. The Americans wanted to block any Soviet ambitions to gain a communist foothold in the Congo and block the followers of Lumumba, whom they considered a Marxist.

In early January 1961 the news got out that Patrice Lumumba had been handed over to the government of Katanga and had been beaten and tortured. As the month rolled on, a rumor began spreading that the prime minister had been executed. No one knew for sure, and in Nebobongo Helen kept busy with her hospital work and wondered, if true, what impact the death of Lumumba would have on the country, especially in the north, where they were located and where Lumumba's support was the strongest.

It wasn't until February 13, 1961, that news of the execution of Lumumba was officially released. According to the report Helen heard on the radio, he'd been executed by Katangese troops near the town of Élisabethville on January 17, 1961. News of his death was followed by more executions of his followers in the Congo. The news also provoked international outrage. The Belgian embassy in Belgrade, Yugoslavia, was attacked by protesters. And in London and New York, violent demonstrations over Lumumba's execution took place.

Three days after the announcement of Lumumba's death, Helen was driving to Wamba to make her rounds, assessing and treating patients at the hospital and the prison. Normally on her trip to Wamba, Jack Scholes rode along with Helen to make sure she arrived safely, but not today. As she drove, Helen watched wearily in the rearview mirror as a police jeep drove up behind her and began honking its horn. The driver raised a hand and motioned for Helen to pull to the side of the road. "You're under arrest!" the officer yelled at her as her pickup truck came to a halt.

"What do you mean?" Helen asked. "What did I do wrong?"

"Ha, you turned right without using your indicator," the police officer replied.

"This is ridiculous," Helen snapped. "I'm the only car on the road. We are in the middle of nowhere. You can't arrest me for that."

Helen felt the cold end of a gun against her ear. "I said you're under arrest," the officer repeated.

Helen stopped talking. She got into the jeep with the policeman, where she sat grim-faced and silent as he drove to the Wamba police station. Every so often

Helen glanced at her watch. She was going to be late for work regardless of what happened at the police station.

At the Wamba police station, the sergeant sitting at the desk looked up at the police officer and asked, "What's this all about?"

Helen jumped in to explain. "I was just . . ." *Wham!* Helen felt a hand slap her across the face. The force of the slap made her teeth throb.

"Don't speak until I tell you to!" the police officer said. "And stand at attention. Have you no respect for authority?"

Helen straightened up and put her hands at her sides.

"Do you think you are better than us?" the officer asked. "That's the sort of thing white colonists were always doing—ignoring traffic signs and thinking they could get away with it. But not now. Now we are a republic. The Congolese are in charge. We demand that you obey our traffic rules. Do you understand?"

Helen understood perfectly. This had nothing to do with not using her turn signal on an empty road. Rather, it was about people who were angry at not having had the power they wanted in the past.

Two long hours passed before the bullying at the hands of the policemen stopped and Helen was allowed to go. She had someone give her a ride back to her truck at the side of the road. As she drove back to Wamba to start her hospital rounds, Helen was sobered. She understood why so many Congolese people hated whites, but she had come to help them and had chosen to stay, even when it was dangerous.

Despite the incident with the police, Helen continued to drive to Wamba twice a week to fulfill her official duties at the hospital and prison. Often, she used the opportunity to stock up on whatever food and goods she could find in town for the Nebobongo hospital and her friends at Pawa.

One day in early March she was pleased to have been able to find and purchase bolts of fabric to make more uniforms for the orphans and student nurses. It was after 10:00 p.m. when she arrived back at Nebobongo, where a nurse and a workman helped unload the pickup. Once everything had been dumped in the front room of her house, Helen decided to leave it there until morning. She was bone-tired and needed sleep.

On her way to bed Helen wandered into the kitchen to get a glass of water. She spotted a plate of food her houseboy must have left out for her. She sat down at the table in front of the plate as her puppy nudged her hand. She picked up a piece of plantain from the plate and nibbled at it before realizing she was too tired to eat. Reaching down Helen gave the rest of the chunk of plantain to the puppy. "There you are," she said. The puppy whimpered for more, and Helen gave in. She placed the plate of food on the floor and headed to bed.

The next morning, when Helen awoke, she could barely lift her head. Waves of nausea swept over her. Turning to look out the window, she noticed her bedroom curtains were gone. She looked around the room. Nothing else was in it except her bed—no chair, no books, no clothes. Then, focusing on her bed, she realized that her pillow and sheets were also missing. During the night it appeared that someone had stripped her house bare. She heard the sound of her houseboy, Benjamin, opening the front door. Then she heard him gasp before he raced into her room. "The puppy's dead!" Benjamin yelled.

Helen turned her head toward him. "Get me Mama Damaris," she groaned.

For the next three days Helen drifted in and out of consciousness. When she was able to speak, the church elders came and asked her questions. What did she remember about the night she was robbed? Had she told anyone she had bought the bolts of cloth? Did she see anyone acting suspiciously? Although Helen could hardly think straight, she tried her best to answer their questions.

When she started to feel better, the elders told her they were convinced that someone had meant to murder her with the plantain, which had been soaked in poisonous berry juice and left on the plate. But the puppy had eaten most of the poison meant for Helen. The thought that someone who lived nearby, or who possibly even worked at the hospital, wanted Helen dead was sobering.

As the remainder of the year went by, and 1962 and 1963 after that, Helen got used to being a target of threats and crimes. Her house was broken into several times, and things she bought to replace stolen items were also stolen. Like everyone else, she adjusted to a new level of jeopardy in everyday life. Yet through it all, the missionary work at Nebobongo flourished. The hospital had grown to have one hundred beds, while the maternity ward had an additional twenty beds, and over five hundred babies a year were born there. Over one hundred young men, along with two young women, had been trained and earned their nursing diplomas. Over one hundred children regularly attended the mission school. Helen loved the challenge of keeping it all running smoothly, even in the face of so many difficulties.

In June 1964, the constantly changing political landscape in the Congo following independence changed yet again. That month, the last of the United Nations peacekeeping troops left the Congo, though many, including Helen, felt they departed leaving the country no safer than when they had arrived. Within weeks of the withdrawal, fighting broke out again. Christophe Gbenye, a one-time friend and political ally of Patrice Lumumba, along with Pierre Mulele and Gaston Soumialot, led a rebellion that captured Stanleyville and large parts of northeastern Congo. Gbenye then established the Marxist-style People's Republic of the Congo, declaring himself to be president.

As the Congo devolved into a new level of lawlessness, Helen joined the other missionaries serving around the Ibambi area in trying to make sense of what was happening. Various shortwave radio channels brought news from the BBC in England and from China, the Soviet Union, and Leopoldville.

While each channel seemed to give wildly differing accounts of what was happening, they all seemed to agree on one thing: Stanleyville had been captured by Gbenye and a group of rebels calling themselves Simbas, or Lions, as the word meant in Swahili.

The Simbas were a fierce group of fighters made up mostly of young men and teens, and even some children. From the radio reports Helen learned that these rebel fighters held many traditional beliefs. They relied upon witches and witch doctors to help them understand what was going on around them. They often went into battle under the influence of drugs and traditional substances. And they believed in "dawa," water which, when ritually applied by a witch doctor to a fighter, left the fighter impervious to bullets from his enemies' guns.

Because Stanleyville was only 220 miles southwest of Ibambi and the Simbas were capturing more territory in the north of the country, the missionaries continued monitoring the radio for news. They also kept a watchful eye out, especially for cars filled with Simba fighters driving on the roads throughout the area.

On Saturday, August 15, 1964, Helen had her first encounter with the Simbas. She was taking an afternoon nap when a uniformed man burst into her house. He started yelling in French about a person having been shot and needing help. Helen's heart lurched. This was exactly what she feared—soldiers with serious, perhaps potentially fatal, battle wounds that she would be expected to repair every time.

A stocky man was carried onto Helen's veranda. He was shirtless and had a white bandage around his shoulder and under his arm. "Has someone seen him already?" she asked.

The uniformed Simba soldier nodded. "We took him to the hospital at Wamba, but they do not have a real doctor. You must look at his wound."

Helen removed the bandages from the man and studied his injury. To her great relief, a bullet had merely grazed his shoulder blade, and it looked to her as if the nurses at Wamba had done a thorough job of cleaning the wound. She swabbed it once more with antiseptic and redressed it.

"Don't move your shoulder too much," she told the patient. "And if it starts to feel hot or you get a fever, come back and see me."

Now that Helen knew she was on the Simbas' radar, she carried out an important task. The pickup truck was too valuable to her and the hospital to let it be taken away without a fight. She marched out to the garage and jacked up the rear axle of the truck. When the wheels were clear of the ground, she unbolted one and took it off. She took that wheel, and the spare wheel, and hid them under her bed. She returned to the pickup truck, lifted the hood, and pulled off the coil lead, without which the engine would have no power.

Helen then went inside and played a round of Scrabble with Florence, who, though she had originally left the Congo during the upheaval following independence, had returned to her work in the maternity ward in the hospital at Nebobongo.

As the Simba rebellion grew in the north of the Congo, all of the mission organizations working in the area faced a quandary: Should their missionaries stay or leave? On August 30, 1964, several American missions ordered their missionaries out of the country. Helen and the other WEC missionaries, including Bill McChesney, an American, stayed on. But for how long?

Snippets of news filtered into Nebobongo. The Simbas had set up in the town of Paulis, about thirty miles due north, where they murdered three thousand people who had supported the national government. They also went into the surrounding villages and encouraged purges, in which every man, woman, and child from the village was interrogated. Anyone who showed signs of not being one hundred percent loyal to the Simbas—or even appeared to one of the Simba witches to be disloyal—was killed on the spot. When Wamba was purged by the Simbas, runners reported that a thousand people had been killed. Helen could only imagine the horror many Congolese people were experiencing at the hands of the Simbas.

Sometimes things were quiet around Nebobongo. At other times there was a rush of activity as cars and trucks filled with gun-waving young men roared past the hospital on their way to a battle somewhere. Sometimes Helen would recognize a car and wonder what had happened to its owner. She had no way of knowing.

By early October 1964, Helen and the staff at Nebobongo were isolated. No one was allowed to travel or even walk down a road without papers, and mail delivery had ceased. All they could do was wait and pray that it would all be over soon.

Simba fighters began stopping off at the hospital more frequently. Sometimes they demanded medical treatment. Other times they came to Helen's house and rifled through all the drawers and cupboards hoping to find money. They also took every electrical device they could get their hands on and taunted the medical staff as they left the hospital workers without vital equipment.

On the night of Thursday, October 29, the Simba rebels returned to Helen's house. This time they demanded to see her husband. She could not convince them that she was not hiding a husband in the house. A group of men tore the place apart, dumping the contents of every drawer and box onto the floor and taking what they wanted. They ordered the two male nurses who were staying in the house with Helen to take the loot to their car.

Left alone with their leader, Helen made an instinctive decision. She ran out the side door and into the night. A half moon shone above as she ran in her bare feet, barely able to make out the tangle of roots along the path. She could hear men crashing through the jungle behind her, yelling drunken curses as they went. A few minutes later Helen could run no farther. She dove under some bushes and covered her hands and feet with her dressing gown. She then put her head down into the mud so that her white skin would not catch the reflection of a flashlight.

Despite her attempt to escape, the men found Helen ten minutes later and dragged her to her feet. She felt a blow from behind as someone struck her with a bat. She tasted blood as two of her back teeth fell out from the blow. She was pushed back along the path to her house. Hugh, one of the nurses, stood waiting to help her. Lieutenant George pushed him out of the way. Hugh pushed back, putting his body between Helen and the lieutenant. Several other Simbas shoved Hugh down the veranda steps to the ground, where they kicked him.

"Now we go to Paulis," Lieutenant George ordered. "You sit beside me," he said, turning to Helen and softening his voice.

Helen recoiled. She was living her worst nightmare. A dark evil had enveloped her.

The rest of the evening and the next day passed in a blur of pain and shock. Helen was driven to the Simbas' local headquarters south of Ibambi and shoved inside. Huddled in a corner of the room, she was able to assess her wounds. Along with the two back teeth that had been knocked out, a third was broken. Helen's body ached, but she didn't think that any of her bones were broken.

Men came and went from the headquarters all night. Some were drunk, some were yelling obscenities, others were threatening each other. To Helen it seemed a place of utter confusion. An hour or so before daybreak, five Catholic nuns, three priests, and a layman from the Ibambi cotton factory were shoved into the room and ordered to sit. Helen dared not make eye contact with them. A half hour later four Greek men joined the group. Helen knew them as local traders and wondered where their wives and children were.

More white people arrived and were crammed into the room—first those from a nearby town, then those from Pawa, including eight nuns, three priests, and Dr. Swertz. Helen was glad to know that the doctor was safe. While he'd refused to talk to Helen when she trained for her Congo medical license, over the years Dr. Swertz and Helen had forged a friendship. The doctor had evacuated the country with other Belgian colonists under armed guard nearly four years before, leaving behind his Congolese wife, who suffered from tuberculosis. Before being evacuated, he had asked Helen to look after his wife, which she did to the best of her ability. As soon as he was able, Dr. Swertz returned to the Congo to be with his wife and take care of her himself. Given the way so many white colonists had used and abused the Congolese, Helen was touched by Dr. Swertz's dedication to his Congolese wife.

The other WEC missionaries from Ibambi arrived and were shoved into the room. Helen longed to hug them, but she dared not move. However, the Simba guards stepped out of the room every few minutes, allowing the prisoners to quickly whisper news to each other. Helen learned that white people across the region were being herded together and taken prisoner. Every so often there was a burst of organization from their Simba captors. Everyone had to hand over his or her passport, and a list of nationalities was drawn up. The Belgians and Americans were separated and threatened with death.

At nine thirty the next morning a four-ton truck pulled up next to the building. All of the captured whites were pushed up onto the back of it. The sun beat down on the truck bed, and soon the stench of closely packed people in the fierce equatorial heat was almost unbearable. As they waited and waited, Helen wondered where the truck had been stolen from.

After much yelling and cursing, the truck engine started, and the vehicle lurched forward. It didn't take Helen long to realize they were headed toward Paulis, where they arrived at two o'clock in the afternoon. The truck horn blasted as the truck pulled up and Simba rebels streamed out of a building to meet it.

After being unloaded from the truck, Helen and the others were ordered to stand under a jacaranda tree. As the Simba rebels separated the men from the women, they yelled and argued among themselves. Helen understood most of what they said but found it hard to believe that any group could be as disorganized as her captors were. Furious that this group of white people had been rounded up, the Simba commander at Paulis demanded to know why. Helen watched as Lieutenant George and the others who had captured them turned from being proud of bringing so many white people to Paulis to being apologetic for their actions. The commander ordered that all the whites be loaded back onto the truck and returned to where they had come from.

Without a word, the group of nuns, priests, Greek traders, doctors, and Protestant missionaries climbed back onto the truck bed and found a place to settle down. Helen wondered if they were really going home, or if they would be overtaken on the road and ordered back to Paulis or somewhere else. She was almost too weary to care.

Chapter 11

Hostage

Helen hadn't expected to see Nebobongo again, until the truck carrying her and the white captives stopped at her house. On the way back from Paulis, the WEC missionaries on the truck decided it would be safer for Helen, Florence, Elaine, and Amy Grant to stay at Ibambi with them. One of the missionaries managed to negotiate for the Simba rebels to stop the truck and wait five minutes at Nebobongo while Helen and the others gathered a few belongings.

When all the WEC missionaries in the area had been offloaded at Ibambi, the local church members did all they could to make them feel comfortable and secure. But back at Ibambi, Helen found it impossible to calm herself down. She tensed up at the sound of every car or truck that rumbled along the road. Would the vehicle keep going, or would it stop, round up the missionaries, and cart them away again? Meanwhile, the local Simbas were alternately cruel and attentive. One day they came and took away the last remaining radio the missionaries relied upon for international coverage of the civil war in the Congo. A few days later they returned it as a "gift." Another time they allowed the Greek traders to give them a goat to cook and eat but then demanded *all* the food the traders had on hand to feed their men. It was impossible to know what was going to happen from one moment to the next.

One night, Helen and the rest of the missionaries at Ibambi were rounded up, arrested, and marched off in one direction before being returned to Ibambi, only to be marched off in the opposite direction. At last they were allowed to return to the mission compound and go back to their rooms.

The weeks dragged on at Ibambi. No letters or newspapers got through to the mission station. The only way Helen and the others stayed informed was through rumors that swept the countryside and news they were able to glean from the radio the Simbas had taken and then returned.

In July 1964, a new national government took over from the previous one, with a mandate to end the regional revolts occurring around the country, including the Simba rebellion in the north. In August, about the same time Helen had her first encounter with the Simba rebels, the Congolese national army—this time supported by white foreign mercenaries (soldiers)—began making some headway against the Simbas. In response, the Simba rebels began taking hostages from among the white population areas under their control.

Several hundred hostages were rounded up and taken to Stanleyville, where they were kept under guard in the Victoria Hotel. A group of Belgian and Italian nuns were also taken hostage by the Simbas and forced to do hard labor for their captors. Helen remembered the rumors that leaked out about how the nuns were brutalized by the Simbas until they had been liberated by the national forces and the mercenaries and flown out of the country to Belgium. Helen decided their liberation probably accounted for how nervous the Simbas became when they heard airplanes flying overhead. They were never sure whether the airplane was about to attack them.

Government forces continued their attacks against the Simbas, killing many of them and liberating areas they controlled. Rumors trickled back to the missionaries at Ibambi that the Simbas were once again rounding up white people and taking them hostage. Helen wasn't surprised. It had always seemed to her to be the inevitable outcome, though she wasn't sure why they needed so many white captives. However, she soon found out.

Several trusted Congolese men from the surrounding area passed along to Helen a rumor they had heard. As the national army, with the support of white mercenaries, began gaining the upper hand against the Simbas, more and more Simba fighters were dying in battle after being hit by enemy bullets. This wasn't supposed to be. Dawa, the ritual sprinkling of water on each fighter by a witch doctor, was supposed to make the men impervious to enemy bullets. The fighters weren't supposed to be able to be killed in battle. But that obviously wasn't the case.

At first the witch doctors couldn't explain why the Simba fighters were dying from enemy bullets. But as they talked among themselves and thought about it, they decided that dawa had lost its power to protect the men from injury and death because of a stronger witchcraft the white mercenary soldiers had brought with them. Also, the white doctors and missionaries were working with the white mercenaries in their witchcraft, giving the national army even more power in their fight against the Simbas.

The only way to break the power of this white magic, the witch doctors said, was to capture as many whites as possible and get rid of them. The Simba leaders had given orders for their fighters to capture even more whites and lock them up. This was a chilling rumor for Helen, who had no doubt the Simbas believed it completely. She just hoped that the national army would beat the Simbas before the rebels returned to Ibambi to take the missionaries prisoner again. But it wasn't to be.

On Saturday morning, November 28, 1964, the inevitable occurred. Around ten o'clock, Helen heard a truck rumbling down the road toward them. Helen, Florence, Elaine, and Amy, and the three Ibambi-based missionaries (Jack and Jessie Scholes and Englishman Brian Cripps, the print shop manager) all hurried into Jack's office and barred the door. Everyone strained to hear what would happen outside the office.

Helen heard the truck doors slam shut and the sound of boots stamping on the gravel. Angry voices soon rose. Some were the voices of Ibambi Christians, who refused to reveal where the missionaries were. But they must have worked it out. A splintering sound was followed by yells and groans as the rebels tried to break down the door to Jack's office. The missionaries all held their breath. There was more beating on the door, until Jack walked over, unlocked the door, and walked out of the office. Brian followed him. Tears stung Helen's eyes as the men exited the office. These two men were willing to take the first blows for them all.

Helen hoped it would all be over quickly, that they wouldn't have to endure torture before they were killed. But the sounds of blows never came. Instead the local Simba leader said to Jack, "You are causing us a lot of trouble. We have orders to take you back to Wamba. You will be safer there. The other Simbas are dangerous. They're out of control. If they find you, they will kill you. Quickly, you must come with us."

Helen was stunned. Were they really being taken to safety, or was it a trap to take them deeper into Simba country where they could be held hostage, killed to weaken the white magic that had overcome the witch doctors' dawa, or used for barter with the government forces?

"Everyone can take one suitcase, a small case, a blanket, and a pillow," the Simba leader announced.

Mechanically, the missionaries moved to collect their few belongings. Helen picked up her luggage and walked wearily to the truck. *How many more rides would there be like this,* she wondered.

Other Congolese who needed a ride to Wamba joined them. Soon the truck was packed with the seven missionaries, twenty-four men, four women, two goats, a basket of chickens, plantains, a drum of palm fat, and assorted boxes and bags and luggage. As they drove along, one of the Simba guards held a hand grenade, pin pulled, ready to throw it at any vehicle that came too close to them.

The truck rolled into Wamba at 6:00 p.m. The long, slow journey in the sweltering sun had taken nearly four hours. The truck drove up to the doors of the Catholic convent, where the women missionaries were ordered out and the men told to remain at the back of the truck. "Where are you taking the men?" Jessie asked.

"To the priest's house," a Simba replied.

Helen and the other four women were ushered inside the convent, where forty-five nuns, some European, some African, sat in silence on the veranda. With them were two white women in regular clothes and five children. No one looked up. The mother superior welcomed the five women and showed them a small cell where they could put their belongings. "I am afraid we are very overcrowded," the mother superior said. "This convent was built to house six nuns, but the Simbas have crammed over forty-five women and children into it."

When a bell rang, Helen and the others followed the nuns to a crowded dining area, where they ate a simple meal of pasta and sauce. That night, the five missionary women from Ibambi settled into their new room—a ten-foot-square nun's cell. The only mattress was allotted to Jessie, since she was the oldest. Helen claimed a spot on the concrete floor and lay down to sleep.

The following morning at breakfast, the nuns asked what had happened to the women missionaries and what news they had from the outside. In exchange, the mother superior told them that many of the Belgian priests at the Sacred Heart of Jesus Church next door had already been killed. In a hushed whisper she described to Helen how Colonel Pierre Olombe, a Simba leader, and his men had arrived at the convent a week before. The colonel was wearing Bishop Wittebols's sash, ring, and cross. "From now on, I am your bishop," he had told the nuns. "Those who disobey me will be in trouble."

The mother superior took a deep breath and then lowered her voice even more. Looking into Helen's eyes she said, "They also killed two male missionaries. I believe they were from WEC. One was an American and one Scottish."

Helen's mouth went dry as she said, "Bill McChesney and Jim Rodger?" She knew that Jim's latest assignment had been in Wamba.

The mother superior nodded. "Yes, I believe those

were their names. The Scottish one refused to say he wasn't an American, so he could stay with the other man who was suffering badly from a beating. In the end, both were then speared."

Helen's stomach churned at the news. She put down her fork and could eat no more. *How much suffering can we take?* she asked herself as she thought of Bill and how she had traveled back to the Congo with him after furlough. Bill had been a dedicated young man with a deep desire to follow God's call to the Congo. And now he and Jim were both martyrs for their faith.

For the next week, the women in the convent were left alone. The missionaries from Ibambi were assigned duties. Helen set and lit the fire in the morning, made coffee at breakfast, and took her turn on the roster clearing the tables and washing the dishes after a meal. She was relieved to discover that the nuns had a well-stocked library. All the books were in French, and she selected one on the life of Saint Teresa to read. It was wonderful to lose herself in the story even for a few minutes before being jolted back to her present reality.

Early on December 10, 1964, one of the missionary women overheard a guard say that mercenary paratroopers had dropped from airplanes into Paulis. It was exciting news, but was it true? Later that morning, Helen was preparing to collect buckets of water from a nearby well. Just as she left the convent with her Simba guard, she saw several trucks pull up. Helen asked to return to see what was going on, but the guard refused. When Helen returned thirty minutes later carrying two buckets of water, she found the convent empty. The other missionary women and the nuns were gone.

"They've been taken to the prison on the colonel's orders," her Simba guard said.

Helen's heart dropped. She dreaded to think about what might be happening to them at the prison, but she dreaded even more being alone with Simba guards at the convent. "Take me to them," she ordered her guard in the most authoritarian voice she could muster. Much to her surprise, her guard nodded and told her to get her things. An hour later, Helen was reunited with the other women. She held out hope that the rumor about the paratroopers was true. Why else would the Simba colonel have moved the women to a more secure location?

Within hours the Protestant missionaries were escorted back to the convent. Over the next few days, the nuns and Belgian women arrived. Helen prayed that their ordeal would soon be over.

As Christmas approached, truckloads of women and children arrived at the convent: Greek traders' wives and children, Protestant missionaries from farther afield, and more nuns, bringing the number of people imprisoned in the convent to over seventy. Somehow, they all decided to do their best to celebrate Christmas. Almost miraculously, the mother superior had managed to keep two turkeys alive in a pen at the back of the convent, and Jessie was assigned to work out the best way to cook them. Lacking any way to duplicate text, Helen typed out forty copies of Christmas carols including "Silent Night" in Swahili and "O Come, All Ye Faithful" in French. The nuns, who met for mass every morning, practiced a special Christmas mass, and small gifts for the children were found and wrapped.

By Christmas Eve, everything was ready, and everyone looked forward to the following day. Late on Christmas Eve, a Simba commander arrived at the convent and announced that the mother superior and four other nuns were to depart with him immediately. Helen looked at the mother superior and wanted to say something, but it was as if she had read Helen's mind. "I know what you're thinking—to be taken away before we celebrate Christmas together. But what can we do? You know what will happen if we resist. Be strong in the Lord."

Helen let out a long sigh. She knew they had no choice in the matter.

The mother superior and the four nuns left before midnight, and by the time Helen lay down to sleep it was early Christmas morning. Yet every ounce of joy she'd been feeling about Christmas had evaporated.

Later that morning, Helen and the other women carried on with their Christmas celebration plans for the sake of the children, but Helen noted that no one seemed to be in a celebratory mood.

Two nights later the Simba commander who had taken away the mother superior and the four nuns showed up at the convent. "You are all going to be evacuated tonight. Get your things now," he ordered.

Their few belongings in hand, the women, along with their children, were herded into the back of a pickup truck. When it was full, the truck drove off, leaving some of the women behind to be picked up later. In all, thirteen women were in the back of the truck, eight Protestant women and five nuns. Clouds hid the moon as the truck's wheels spat up red dirt and drove away. Helen knew they were in a dangerous situation—she and twelve other exhausted women in the hands of five Simba rebels who were being chased by the national army and foreign mercenaries. They had no way to predict what the rebels might do if they felt cornered.

All Helen knew was that they were being transferred north to Mungbere, about one hundred miles away. However, not long after midnight, the truck pulled off the road at Betongwe, a tiny settlement about twenty-five miles from Mungbere. Helen wondered why they had stopped.

"This place belonged to a Belgian planter I knew," one of the nuns whispered.

"Get down," one of the guards yelled. "Get out of the truck now!"

"Why?" Helen asked. "What is here? Can't we go on to Mungbere?"

The Simba fighter struck her. She climbed down from the truck.

When the women had climbed out of the truck, they were led to a large bungalow set back a little from the road. Inside they were told to sit down on the concrete floor with their backs to the wall. All they had was one hurricane lantern to light the room.

News soon got around Betongwe that a group of white women were at the bungalow. At dawn a mob of local men and women gathered outside the house jeering and thumping on the doors. Helen was sure that this was the end for them all. However, the Simba sergeant major in charge of the area arrived with several guards and forced the crowd back before they could do anything. To Helen's surprise, the sergeant major seemed like an honorable man. He left guards posted at the bungalow while he went to organize some food for the women.

At lunchtime, seven more Belgian women and nine children arrived. Soon afterward, eighteen nuns and five men joined them. A second truckload of captives that came by did not unload its cargo. Instead, five nuns, along with two women and four children, were taken from the bungalow and shoved into the truck, which then lumbered off down the road. Helen could make no sense of the way they were being transported around.

Soon after the truck departed, the Simba sergeant major showed up to feed the women rice and peanuts and to assure them that they would be protected throughout the night.

Helen slept little that night, and by the time the sun came up she felt on the verge of mental and physical collapse. She didn't know how much more she could take of not knowing if she would be alive by the time the sun set.

Chapter 12

Tangible Love

Helen wasn't sure what time it was, perhaps an hour after sunrise, when a new group of Simba guards arrived to watch over them. These new guards were not as disciplined as those who had watched them through the night. Before she could properly assess how they should react to the new guards, the bungalow reverberated with the sound of airplanes and several thunderous blasts. The Simba guards became agitated.

They then began forcing the captives back into the main room of the bungalow. It was easy for Helen to see the Simbas were scared.

As the sounds of aircraft and explosions continued, the Simba guards forced them all into a smaller room. Helen was on high alert. The situation was the most volatile yet. The Simbas were out of control. Helen was sure that if one Simba fired his gun, they would all open fire and the prisoners would be dead within seconds.

Then Helen heard another sound, the sound of revving engines and vehicles traveling at high speed, accompanied by a rhythmic *pop-pop-pop* sound. "A machine gun," one of the captives gasped.

At the word machine gun, Helen saw the fear in the Simbas' eyes grow. Again, they seemed to have no idea how they should respond. Unexpectedly, they turned and fled from the bungalow.

Outside Helen could hear the machine-gun fire pick up. "Get down, flat on the floor!" she yelled. Simbas screamed and shouted outside. Helen heard the truck and jeep engines grow closer. She heard more gunfire and then the sound of the boots of men rushing toward the bungalow. Moments later the door was kicked down. Men with rifles in hand stood ready to fire, but they were white men—foreign mercenaries. The captives were safe. Tears streamed down Helen's cheeks. She could barely believe it. She'd been ready to die at the hands of the Simbas, but now here she was, surrounded by men who had come to rescue her and the others.

After a few minutes Helen regained her composure. By then it was time to leave. The trucks and jeeps, accompanied by two large helicopters, Helen learned, had attacked Mungbere just after dawn and freed the prisoners the Simbas held there.

The freed prisoners were told they could take

nothing, except, perhaps, something the size of a small briefcase. The trucks were too full already. "We're not out of the woods yet," Lieutenant Joe Wepener, leader of the group of foreign mercenaries, said. The lieutenant said they had one hundred miles to go to make it back to Paulis before dark. Helen grabbed one of the young children and carried her to the truck, which was already overloaded with anxious people. Arms reached out for the child, and then for Helen. She heaved herself up and over people until she was sitting on someone's knees near the middle of the group.

"Hello, Helen!" she heard a man's voice say. She looked around and realized she was sitting on Brian Cripps's knees. More tears ran down her cheeks. She had thought she would never again see any of the other male missionaries from Ibambi.

Soon the trucks and the jeeps with their mounted machine guns sped away from Betongwe. As they drove along, the gunners machine-gunned patches of jungle and long grass where they thought Simba fighters might be lying in ambush for them.

Thankfully they encountered no ambush along the way and arrived at Paulis just as the sun was beginning to set. Safely at Paulis, everyone bathed, a delight Helen hadn't enjoyed in many days. This was followed by a thanksgiving service.

After the service was over, Helen stretched out on a soft bed to sleep. She thought back to just a few hours before when she was sure the Simbas would kill her, yet here she was, alive and safe. "God, forgive me for all the moments I doubted that this time would come," she prayed as she drifted off to sleep.

The following morning the freed captives were flown to Leopoldville, and from there to Amsterdam, Holland, and then to London.

Back in England, although on the inside Helen felt cold and distant, on the outside she hugged her family and friends, spoke at Sunday schools, and told parts of her story to her mother. But underneath she was numb with grief and shock over what she'd experienced in the Congo at the hands of the Simbas. When a reporter asked if she would ever go back to the Congo, Helen replied, "When you've just escaped from the lion's cage at dinnertime, you don't go back to offer yourself as dessert!"

Helen set out on a tour of Great Britain, often speaking at two engagements a day. It was a relief for her to have something to keep her busy, something that took her mind off what had happened in the Congo. She also completed an eight-week course on midwifery and women's health, and spent a lot of time with her mother, who now was quite crippled with arthritis.

In August 1965, Helen attended a Bible youth camp near Anglesey, Wales, with her old friend Major Leonard Moules, who was now the secretary of WEC International. Just being with Len and other members of WEC made Helen realize that these people were her family. She belonged with them, and she belonged in the Congo. Quietly, she began making inquiries about going back as a missionary doctor. At first Len thought she was joking. Why, he asked, would she want to return to the place where she'd been treated so badly? In answer to this question, Helen showed him some of the letters she'd recently received from the people there.

One of the letters was from John Mangadima. He had been told that Helen and the other missionary women from Nebobongo had all been killed. He was stunned to learn that they had been rescued. In his letter to Helen he wrote about the damage and destruction inflicted on the hospital and how it was almost impossible to get any drugs or medical supplies. He ended his letter by telling Helen that many young men were waiting for her to return to teach them nursing. "We don't really expect you to come back after all you have suffered from our people," John wrote, "but if God should persuade you, we will never cease to thank Him and to love you and care for you as never before."

Mama Damaris wrote to tell Helen about how she had kept many babies alive while hiding out in the jungle. She too urged Helen to return to Nebobongo and offered an "unlimited supply" of love if she did.

Bebesi, Helen's head carpenter at Nebobongo, wrote to say that one of the exterior mud brick walls of Helen's old house had been blown out. He planned to have it repaired and new shutters made for the windows so the house would be ready for her return.

After reading these and other letters, Len told Helen that he understood why she wanted to return.

He also began making inquiries as to who else from the mission team might be thinking about returning.

Although Helen had been evacuated from the Congo and the Simbas all but beaten by government troops, the political crisis in the country continued. The faction-riddled national government in Leopoldville was virtually paralyzed. On November 25, 1965, Helen heard on the BBC that Joseph-Desiré Mobutu had seized political power in the country as he'd done five years before. Mobutu declared that the purpose of his bloodless coup d'etat was to end political deadlock in the Congo. He declared a state of emergency and assumed near absolute power in the country, promising that in five years democracy would be restored and the country would enjoy political and economic stability. The United States and other Western governments declared their support for Mobutu's new government. It was hoped that this new régime would mark the end of the political crisis that had gone on since the Congo's independence from Belgium. Helen certainly hoped so. It was time for the country to move on and begin developing its resources and infrastructure.

Fifteen months after being evacuated from the Congo, Helen boarded the *Kenya Castle* bound for Mombasa, Kenya, on the first leg of her return journey to the Congo. Traveling with her were Jessie Scholes and Lillie Cripps. Both their husbands had flown on ahead to make sure it was safe enough for their missionary work to resume.

On March 14, 1966, Helen wrote in her diary,

> At last we are on our way. . . . I find that HE has not taken away fear. At moments, I am deeply fearful, and wonder why on earth I'm going back. . . . Areas are still under rebel domination. Then too, I am very conscious that WORK awaits me—perhaps half a million Congolese in the Paulis area who have not seen a doctor for 18 months. I have said this easily, almost casually, at meetings, but my heart pounds if I pause to think what it may mean.

Now that she was on a ship and away from the bustle of visiting friends and family in England, Helen had time to think and pray. A question she wrestled with was what to do about the nurse training program. The idea of training hundreds of Congolese Christian men and women to tend to the basic health care needs of their fellow citizens made far more sense to her than trying on her own to reach everyone in need. But there was a problem, and as far as Helen could see, it was only going to get worse. Although the nurses she trained passed their exams and did good work, the nursing program itself had never gained national accreditation because the medical facilities in the jungle were too primitive.

Before she was evacuated from the Congo, the government at the time had made it even harder for jungle hospitals to receive credentials. Without them, nursing graduates who trained in the program could not work in government hospitals. Five Protestant mission groups were working in the Congo, and Helen knew that none of them had accredited medical workers, even though some had doctors and qualified staff. Given this, Helen wondered if she should continue trying to get accreditation by raising money to build a more Western-style hospital in Nebobongo.

Or was there another way to deal with the issue? Before the Simba rebellion, there had been talk among the mission groups about banding together to build one large, well-equipped hospital that would serve all of eastern Congo. If the mission groups pooled their resources and staff, they would have a better chance of getting full accreditation from the government. Helen wondered whether she should leave Nebobongo and commit herself to becoming the training director if the new hospital went ahead. Or had the crisis in the Congo provided an opportunity to do something bigger and more useful? Since Helen didn't yet have the answers to these questions, she felt the need to investigate them further before committing to again being the permanent doctor at Nebobongo.

The voyage aboard the *Kenya Castle* to Mombasa took two weeks. After docking, it took another five stressful days to get paperwork stamped, supplies through customs, and arrangements made for those supplies to be forwarded to Ibambi by rail and truck. Once this was done, Lillie flew on ahead to the Congo while Jessie and Helen set out overland in a brand-new Land Rover pulling a trailer. The Land Rover had been outfitted for use as an ambulance, and the trailer was packed with every sort of medical equipment imaginable—all a gift from hundreds of well-wishers in England. Helen knew she would find good use for it all when she got back to Nebobongo.

Once they crossed into the Congo, though, Helen's heart sank as she drove along the red dirt roads, stopping at roadblocks every thirty miles or so. She would have to get out of the Land Rover, show her papers to the men manning the roadblock, and explain what two white women were doing alone in the jungle. To make matters worse, most of the men who stopped them were surly and drunk, and they brought back to her terrible memories of her time as a captive of the Simbas. In fact, Helen began to wonder if she really could go back to missionary work. Had she been too affected by her previous experiences at the hands of the Simbas to return? Still, she had a vehicle to deliver. As she drove on, she contemplated leaving the country as soon as she could. The idea of again living in the African jungle scared her and made her feel vulnerable in a way she never wanted to feel again.

After driving fifteen hundred miles from the east coast of Africa, Helen pulled the Land Rover and trailer into Ibambi in the heart of the continent. It was Easter Sunday, April 10, 1966, and a crowd of about three thousand people were gathered at Ibambi for Easter services. When they saw Helen arrive with the Land Rover, they flocked around her, Jessie, and the vehicle, singing and cheering and welcoming them back. To Helen's surprise she found tears welling from her eyes and flowing down her cheeks. For the moment, her thoughts and fears about being back in Africa subsided. She sensed from the crowd a real feeling of connection, as if these were her people and this was where she belonged.

After the rousing welcome at Ibambi, two days later Helen drove on to Nebobongo, where she received another warm and heartfelt greeting from the local Congolese. Parts of Nebobongo resembled things she'd seen in London during the Second World War. Bullet holes were everywhere—in walls, roofs, doors, and windows. Many of the buildings seemed beyond repair. Helen stood looking at her house. Although it had been badly damaged, it still stood. In fact, great strides had been taken to repair the house ahead of her arrival. The smashed brick wall had been rebuilt, and the office and a bedroom inside had been stripped and repairs were under way. However, all the repairs in one bedroom and the kitchen were complete, providing Helen with a place to sleep and eat.

The political divisions since independence and the Simba rebellion had wrought destruction to all manner of structures throughout the region. The destruction had had a devastating effect on the people, who now seemed to have nothing. During Helen's earlier time serving as a missionary among the Congolese, the people wore Western-style clothes. Now everyone was dressed in rags or coverings made from pounded leaves. When she visited the school, Helen saw no books, pens, or paper. The children wrote their lessons on bark slabs using scrub-thorns as pencils or wrote in the dirt with a stick. The teachers had no blackboards or textbooks and taught by talking about only things they could remember.

As she toured Nebobongo and the surrounding area, Helen saw that the most immediate needs among the people were food, clothing, and warm blankets. And the needs kept growing. Hundreds of refugees in the area who had fled the rebellion were coming out from the places deep in the jungle where they had been hiding. Their eyes were glazed over, they had potbellies, and their hair had a ginger-colored tinge, all signs of severe malnutrition. Helen knew that John Mangadima had done much to keep things running in her absence from Nebobongo. He told her that many of the people had died, since their condition was beyond any help they were able to receive at the hospital.

Helen walked the hospital wards. Everything from drugs and dressings to laboratory equipment that John had managed to save had run out a long time ago. Just about everything else in the hospital had been stolen or destroyed by the Simbas. Because the surgery had no scissors, operations were carried out using razor blades without anesthetic.

The good news was that Helen had returned with a large trailerload of drugs and medical equipment. Soon large cans filled with all sorts of needed drugs were unloaded along with tins of gauze, cotton wool, and rolls of bandages. Wooden cupboards containing microscopes were lifted from the trailer, as were new basins for cleanup, surgical instruments, an autoclave, new stretchers, and other items necessary to the smooth running of a medical facility in the African jungle.

Lying in her bed in her old house the first night was an unnerving experience for Helen. Fear gripped her, paralyzing her as memories of the Simbas flooded her thoughts, confirming that she couldn't stay in Africa. She thought she'd managed to stuff away those memories, but here they were, wreaking havoc in her heart and mind. Yet as she lay there trying to deal with the flashbacks, she noticed that behind them was something soft and gentle, something that whispered to her spirit that being back in Africa was exactly the right place for her. That sweet gentleness was manifested in the warm and enthusiastic welcome the local Congolese had given her. It was something Helen knew she needed to focus on.

Over the next couple of days more people came to personally welcome Helen back. She noted that with tears in their eyes many of them apologized for the way she had been treated by the Simbas. People told her that the Simbas' attitude toward her wasn't the attitude of other Congolese in the area who'd been touched in spiritual and physical ways by her. Helen was their missionary, and they were glad to have her back.

Four days after returning to Nebobongo, Helen set out for Leopoldville, the Congo's capital, whose name had just been changed to Kinshasa. In Kinshasa she needed to work on getting a new resident's visa and obtaining the right license plates and paperwork for the Land Rover and trailer.

After accomplishing her goals in Kinshasa, Helen flew to Bunia in the northeast of the country near Lake Albert. On her arrival at Bunia, about two hundred miles east of Nebobongo, Dr. Carl Becker from the Africa Inland Mission (AIM) met her at the airport. Helen was delighted to see him. Dr. Becker was a legend in Africa. The seventy-year-old American and his wife, Marie, had served in the Congo for thirty-five years. Dr. Becker had a reputation for being a brilliant surgeon with a wonderful bedside manner.

Dr. Becker was working at the Bunia clinic for a week, where Helen assisted him as he performed surgery. During their time together, the two talked about their vision for missionary medical work in the Congo. Helen was amazed at how similar their dreams were: three ministries—a large, modern hospital, a fully accredited nurse training school, and a "flying doctor" service. The flying doctor service would take doctors and nurses to remote clinics and bring back seriously ill patients from the jungle for testing or surgery.

Dr. Becker drove Helen thirty miles west from Bunia to Nyankunde. He showed her the hospital wing he'd begun building on forty acres of land nestled on a hillside along a grassy valley dotted with glades of trees. The wing would be a part of a larger hospital serving five mission agencies working in the region. By the time Helen left Nyankunde, she was sure she would be joining Dr. Becker in this venture. He would run the hospital, and she would head up the training center.

Having the opportunity to train hundreds of Christian nurses to go out and serve throughout the Congo, including at Nebobongo, was too good an opportunity for Helen to pass up. It was an exciting prospect, one she felt some urgency about. At the pace Dr. Becker was building the hospital, work on establishing the training facility needed to get started sooner rather than later so that enough trained people would be available to staff it. Helen looked forward to her new future, but first she needed to return to Nebobongo and explain to the church and the other missionaries there that she would be leaving them. She knew that they desperately needed a doctor and that they loved her. In fact, the locals' tangible love for her, manifested in the way they had asked for Helen's forgiveness on behalf of both themselves and the Congolese people for the things the Simbas had done to her, is what had changed her mind about staying in Africa.

Helen returned to Nebobongo by car, truck, and any other vehicle that was able to take her part of the journey. Once she arrived, she gathered the medical staff and church elders together to discuss the vision she and Dr. Becker had for the future. As she had guessed, it was hard for them to imagine letting their doctor go. As Helen answered their questions, however, they warmed to the idea, especially when she promised to return twice a year once they built an airstrip for a small airplane. Besides, she would be leaving the hospital in Nebobongo in the capable hands of John, whom they already knew and trusted.

Before moving on, rather than return to Nyankunde right away, Helen wanted to do what she could for the local people, many of whom were in dire need of food and clothing. On May 7, 1966, Helen once again set out for Kinshasa, where she visited everyone she thought she could help. Ten days later, Helen watched two trucks being loaded with sixty bales of blankets and clothes, sacks of bulgur, 150 cartons of milk powder, and enough school supplies for the fifteen local schools in the area. The fifteen tons of supplies would be loaded onto a barge the next day and taken up the Congo River to Stanleyville. They would be taken by train to Paulis and from there by truck to Nebobongo. The truck drivers told her the whole journey for the goods would take about six to ten weeks. Knowing that lives depended upon the supplies arriving soon, Helen hoped it would be sooner rather than later.

Three weeks later, Helen traveled back to Nebobongo to give everyone there the good news about the supplies being shipped to them. She also got back to work, since there was a lot to be done. The hospital needed to be equipped with new supplies Helen had brought from Great Britain, and Helen had patients waiting to be seen.

As she looked toward the new nurses' training facility at Nyankunde, Helen had to find the right students. She wanted to fill forty-eight spots, thirty-six with new students and twelve with students whose education had been interrupted by the rebellion. Helen sent out invitations to the missionary schools and centers, seeking young men and women with at least three years of schooling who were interested in studying nursing. She also tracked down as many of the students as she could who had been in training before the rebellion and invited them to take the entrance exams to see if they qualified to start as second-year students.

Some people told Helen to slow down, to take a year to think and plan, but Helen felt an urgency to get the nursing program going. Despite the lack of housing and classrooms for the students, Helen wanted to seize the opportunity while she could. The question was, Would the students be willing to share her vision and start with nothing?

Chapter 13

This Was What She Loved

Students for the new medical training school were told to arrive in Nyankunde on August 8, 1966. The first students to arrive were muddy and tired from hitchhiking rides on trucks through three hundred miles of jungle. They had gotten muddy from having to get out and push the vehicles through creeks and up boggy hillsides along the way. As the day went on, other students arrived from different directions. The students were all between ages eighteen and twenty, and each student had at least three years of high-school education. They were all elite students, among the most-educated young people in the country.

By late afternoon, twenty-two students had arrived, twenty men and two women, representing nine tribes and language groups. A group of twelve students from Nebobongo had not yet arrived. Helen wasn't surprised. Fighting was taking place between rebels and National Army forces in the jungle between Nyankunde and Nebobongo. The students would arrive when they knew it was safe to make the journey. That night, as dusk fell across the valley, Helen gathered everyone in a courtyard near the under-construction hospital and officially welcomed them to Nyankunde.

"Where is our college, Madam?" Manessa asked after the welcome.

Helen tried to avoid looking any of the students in the eye as she waved her hand toward a patch of shoulder-height elephant grass on the far side of the hospital structure. "Over there," she said.

The students peered at the patch of grass.

"And the dormitories?" another student asked.

"There too," Helen replied.

"I don't see anything," the student said.

Helen took a deep breath. "Well, as you know we've had over two years of civil war here in the north of the country. Because that has made it difficult to organize buildings, we must make a start ourselves. I know the situation is not ideal, but together we can build something for you and the future of your country." Without stopping for comment, Helen launched into a description of where things would go: first the temporary classrooms and homes, and then the permanent dormitories, classrooms, laboratories, library, dining hall, and playing field.

Some students grumbled. Others stared blankly. Helen thought back to the last meeting she'd had with the local church leaders and hospital staff in Nyankunde. Even though significant financial and accreditation issues had to be worked through, the one thing the church leaders predicted Helen would find impossible to do was convince the students to do physical labor. The leaders explained that many of the new students were the pride of their tribes, sent off for medical training, not to build classrooms and dormitories.

Helen wondered whether she'd been too confident in her approach. "I can see you have questions," she told the students. "You've come here because you want to serve God as medical workers. The first step in reaching that goal is building dormitories and classrooms. I estimate it will take us three months to do so. Then we can start learning. I know it will be hard. I know it's not what you expected. But I promise you this: if you will build, I will teach you all I know. You will be doing this not only for yourselves but also as a ministry to every student who comes here after you."

More grumbling among the students followed.

"Discuss this among yourselves," Helen challenged them. "Meet me back here in this courtyard at six thirty tomorrow morning to tell me if you are willing to build with me."

Helen spent much of the night praying. The morning meeting in the courtyard would be a critical moment. If the students rejected the idea of building their own facilities, the whole notion of setting up a medical training school would be over, not just for this year but probably for good. Helen wasn't sure which way the students would go. She could see that most of them felt entitled to respect because of their educational achievements thus far. However, she could see no other way to get the training school up and running without the students' help.

The next morning Helen arrived at the courtyard at six twenty. It was raining lightly. She stood and waited. By six thirty no one had shown up. The students were being housed temporarily in the village primary-school classrooms, since it was school vacation time. She looked in the direction of the classrooms, but no one was coming. She dragged concrete blocks into place and laid planks across them to provide seating for the students. Helen then sat down in her camp chair, opened an umbrella, and began reading her Bible passage for the day, which consisted of about twelve Bible verses. After that she read on to the end of the chapter, then to the end of the book. By now it was eight forty-five. The students, if they were coming, were over two hours late.

Just as she was about to give up, Helen saw a student walking up the path. Then she saw another and another. She tried to look like as if she'd been expecting them all along and that they were not late.

The students sat on the planks in front of her. "It's good to see you," Helen said. "I thought we would start the day with a hymn, a short Bible reading, and prayer before we divide into groups and get to work."

The students sat silently, almost sullenly, Helen thought. With false cheerfulness, she led them in a hymn, read some Bible verses, and prayed. Then she divided the young men into three groups and asked each group to choose a leader. One group was then given axes to cut down gum trees from a glade about five miles away. The wood from the gum trees would be used for the main beams of the buildings. Members of the second group were given hoes with which to clear the dormitory site. The last group received scythes to slash down the long elephant grass to make a playing field and vegetable garden. The students took the implements and set to work.

Helen marched off with the young men going to fell the gum trees. She had a hunch they might have the most difficulty, and they did. Few of them had ever used an axe or a machete, and their hands blistered quickly. The members of this group were so exhausted by the end of the day that none of them, including Helen, could face walking the five miles back to the hospital. They lay down among the felled trees to sleep. As she drifted off to sleep, Helen's heart beat with excitement. This was what she loved. This was what she always felt her calling to serve in Africa was all about: leading the pioneering effort to establish new missionary endeavors, especially ones like the nurses' training school whose aim was to minister both physically and spiritually to locals and build something of substance for the nation.

After a good night's sleep among the trees and under the stars, Helen and the boys arrived back at the hospital site just after dawn.

It didn't take long for the young men to toughen up, and soon the outlines of buildings began to emerge from the red earth. Setbacks occurred along the way: several of the students became seriously ill with malaria or typhoid fever, the wet season arrived with a seventeen-day deluge, and misunderstandings arose between students from different tribal groups.

Despite the setbacks, after three months the temporary medical training college buildings were two-thirds complete, far enough along for classes to begin the following week. Helen knew it was time for her to make good on her promise that if the students built, she would teach. Work stopped on Saturday, October 29, 1966. The national flag of the Republic of the Congo was raised, hymns were sung, and speeches were given as thirty-six young men in blue-and-green uniforms stood at attention beside three women in blue-and-white striped dresses.

Helen was delighted when seven days later, eleven students from Nebobongo arrived. With them was Basuana Bernard, his wife, and their five children. Basuana had previously been the chaplain and administrator of a missionary primary school and had volunteered to be the training school administrator. Helen was relieved to hand over to him many of the practical matters, such as feeding the students and arranging their paperwork.

Another important person arrived about the same

time. Liliane Fuchsloch was a Swiss nurse who'd been a community nurse and midwife in Nyankunde for ten years. Liliane served with an Open Brethren missionary organization and was returning from a furlough. She had agreed to return to Nyankunde and work alongside Helen as she launched the medical training school. Helen was glad to have Liliane around. Not only was she a good teacher, but also she was able to help with myriad details that needed to be taken care of as the medical training facility became a functioning reality.

On Thursday, November 3, 1966, three last students arrived for the training school from Kisangani, as Stanleyville was now called. The three new arrivals were given supplies and allocated beds in the dormitory. Although they were unaware of it, Helen noted the contrast between these three students and the arrival of the first students at the beginning of August. She showed the new arrivals around the property, pointing out both the medical training buildings still under construction and the various hospital structures still being built. She explained to the three new students how the entire student body was required to spend part of each week helping with the construction. The young men scowled at the news and asked Helen how much she would be paying them an hour. They also wanted to know about the quality of the food served and whether they also had to take turns working in the garden.

Helen's heart sank at their remarks. "These buildings have been built by your fellow students," she said. "They didn't get paid, and neither will you. We're building something here that will allow you to become medical workers and be a blessing to your country for generations to come. If God has called you to be a medical worker, this is the only college in the region offering such courses. If He has not called you, I suggest you leave before we go through the trouble of formally enrolling you. Meet me back here in two hours to tell me what you have decided."

An hour later someone reported to Helen that the new students had already left campus with their bags. As she thought about the response of these three young men, Helen was even more grateful for the first batch of students who'd been willing to adjust their expectations and work hard to build the training school. They could have just as easily walked away.

Slowly, month by month, year by year, more students came to Nyankunde to attend the medical training school. When they weren't studying or working in the hospital wards, they laid bricks and hoisted beams into position as permanent buildings took shape. Of course, they faced many challenges and frustrations along the way, but Helen persevered until the medical training school was running smoothly.

With the medical training school up and running, Helen turned her attention to developing the third aspect of ministry that would tie the new hospital and teaching facility together and allow them to reach out across northern Congo. The third ministry function was a flying doctor service that could take physicians and nurses to remote clinics and seriously ill patients to the Nyankunde hospital for further tests or surgery. Missionary Aviation Fellowship (MAF) already worked in the Congo using pilots and small aircraft to service missionaries situated in remote locations.

Like everything else connected with building the hospital and the training school, making the flying doctor service a reality required a lot of work. Yet it was the kind of pioneering work Helen loved. She entered into discussions with MAF about their airplanes and pilots ferrying doctors to remote clinics in the jungle. For a week the Nyankunde hospital doctor would work with the nursing graduates from the medical training school who manned the clinics full-time. Once she received MAF's approval of the flying doctor proposal, Helen got the exact requirements for the length, width, and desirable location of airstrips and set about meeting with local groups to convince them to supply manpower to clear and level their own runways. She made several visits back to Nebobongo to encourage the Christians there to get behind the project.

In Nebobongo, John Mangadima, who was training to become the director of the medical clinic, worked with Helen to make sure everything got done. The response of the locals at Nebobongo encouraged others to do the same in their villages to support the nurses and medical clinics.

Through Helen's prayer and unwavering commitment to the project, the time arrived for the aerial service to begin. Each Monday an MAF airplane would land at Nyankunde to transport a doctor from the main hospital, along with a supply of drugs and medical equipment, to a clinic or a smaller hospital such as the one at Nebobongo. The airplane would then fly on, leaving the doctor behind for five days, during which time the doctor completed about thirty or forty surgeries. During the five days, the doctor stayed in constant contact with the main hospital in Nyankunde via two-way radio, allowing him or her to consult with surgeons and specialists about a patient's condition. Those patients who needed additional care were flown to the Nyankunde hospital after five days when the MAF airplane came to pick up the doctor.

On the following Monday, MAF would ferry a different doctor from Nyankunde to another of the five main remote medical centers dotted across the area and run by various mission agencies working in northeast Congo. Each of these clinics and small hospitals supported eight to ten or more smaller clinics farther out in the jungle, like the model Helen had pioneered at Nebobongo over a decade before.

Helen breathed a sigh of relief as the new pattern for health care across northern Congo began to work as planned. Where she saw friction points in the system, she tinkered and made small adjustments to alleviate problems and hone the system to run better.

When doctors began flying into Nebobongo regularly, Helen was delighted to learn that John was able to assist them in surgery. In fact, John was soon competent enough to perform emergency operations on his own. Eighteen years had passed since he had come to Helen in late 1953 and asked her to train him as a doctor. Though still technically a nurse, for all practical purposes, and in the eyes of his people, John did the work of a doctor, and not just any doctor, but a skilled surgeon.

By 1973 the last piece of the puzzle fell into place for Helen. Getting it into place had been a long and sometimes tortuous journey. This final piece was gaining official recognition and licensing by the Congolese government. At times Helen thought she had everything taken care of to gain the approval she sought, only to have the government change the rules at the last minute. These changes had undone her many hours of hard work, such as the time she had amassed all the necessary paperwork only to discover that the government had accepted a new standard for how nurses were to be housed.

Going forward, all hospitals and nursing facilities in the country were to provide nurses with individual rooms in which to live that included an indoor flushing toilet. Helen could scarcely believe it. The new standard had originated in Europe, where it made sense, but not in Africa, where few people slept in individual rooms and most people were unfamiliar with flushing toilets and how to use them. Nonetheless, Helen set her sights on modifying the dormitory rooms and installing a flushing toilet in each one. As far as Helen was concerned, it was expensive, time-consuming, and annoying but had to be done.

Following this pattern, Helen inched toward receiving recognition and licensing until she had overcome the barriers she faced and received what she wanted.

By fall 1973 Helen knew she needed a break. The medical training school was now officially recognized by the government, which also began subsidizing the wages of the nurses and doctors at Nyankunde. And MAF's airplanes were making the dream a reality by allowing Christian nursing graduates to return to primitive jungle villages to take care of local medical needs while still having access to and support from a large modern hospital and highly skilled staff.

Much more needed to be done to grow the hospital and medical training school, but the pioneering work was over. Through grit, determination, and God's help, Helen had brought a dream to reality where there had once been nothing. As she came to the end of her time in Nebobongo establishing the hospital and ring of outlying clinics, she felt it was time to turn her heart toward England. Her mother was now quite ill. Helen longed to take some of the burden from her brother and sisters who had been caring for their mother. Helen also had been ill, having recently been hospitalized with various recurrences of tropical diseases. It was now time for a break, but Helen could not imagine leaving the training school unless it was left in good hands. She prayed God would send someone to take over her role.

Within weeks of Helen's decision to leave, a pair of young doctors, English surgeon Philip Wood and his new wife, Nancy, a Canadian general practitioner, volunteered to take over. Helen was thrilled. Nancy had volunteered at the hospital several times when she was single, and she spoke perfect French. The couple were an answer to prayer. Helen would be leaving what she'd pioneered at Nyankunde in capable hands.

At the end of September 1973, Helen boarded an airplane for England. She didn't know what her future held as the plane took off and left the Congo, or Zaire, as it was now officially called. As the jungles and savannah of Africa passed below, Helen quietly thanked God that she had been able to play a role in bringing health care and Christian hope to millions of people.

Chapter 14

Living Stones

The first thing Helen did upon her return to Great Britain was to take her ailing mother on holiday in Cornwall. After the vacation, the leaders of WEC–UK offered the two women a place to live at their headquarters. Helen gladly accepted the invitation, and soon she and her mother were loved figures around the place. The arrangement allowed Helen to care for her mother and still be able to speak to high school and student groups about WEC's missionary work. Staying at the headquarters also gave Helen a place and the opportunity to finish writing her book *He Gave Us a Valley*, a follow-up to her first book, *Give Me This Mountain*. The first book, written during her previous furlough, told the story of her work at Nebobongo and the experience of living through the Simba rebellion.

One year passed quickly, and then another. Helen was invited by WEC's USA branch to speak at meetings across the United States and Canada during September 1975. She accepted the invitation and set out for the United States. While she was away, her mother died. Upon her return to England after the speaking engagement, Helen was diagnosed with breast cancer. She underwent surgery and began a long period of recovery. While she recovered, her brother, Bob, his wife, Ione, and their boys visited her. They had left Natal and were now living back in England. With a grin on his face, Bob told Helen that he and Ione were at last free to reveal the secret work they had been involved in during World War II. They had both worked at Bletchley Park, using their math skills to break enemy codes, first German and then Japanese. After being kept secret by the government for thirty years, the nature of what went on at Bletchley Park had recently been declassified. For the first time in their lives Bob and Ione could tell others about their wartime secret. Helen had suspected that Bob had been doing something like that. Now she knew for sure, and she was proud of him. Bob had always had an uncanny knack with mathematics.

By June 1976, Helen was feeling well enough to ask the question, What's next? Should she return to missionary work in the Congo or somewhere else in Africa, or should she stay in England? As was Helen's habit when she wasn't sure what to do, she prayed about it and asked a number of her friends to also pray. After praying, Helen and some of those praying for her felt that God wanted her to stay in Great Britain rather than return to Africa. With her second book now completed and in the hands of her publisher, Helen embarked upon writing another book, this one about WEC's core beliefs and values. She also volunteered to spend a year in Glasgow, Scotland, working with the WEC Missionary Training College, where she spent her time lecturing students and helping out in the office.

Helen was grateful for the time in Glasgow. It allowed her to prepare for her next big step. She had agreed to speak at the upcoming Urbana conference, a large Christian student missions event sponsored by InterVarsity Christian Fellowship, and to help in the United States on the campus of the University of Illinois in Urbana–Champaign. Having agreed to participate, Helen started wondering why she'd done so. Other speakers at the conference included outstanding Christian leaders, such as Billy Graham, John Stott, and Elisabeth Elliot.

Even though she felt herself far outside the league of the main speakers at the conference, at the end of December 1976 Helen flew to Chicago and then traveled on to Urbana for the five-day conference. The event was an eye-opener for Helen as seventeen thousand university students from across North America and around the world came to listen to and be challenged by various missions speakers. When it was her turn to speak, Helen stood before the crowd and delivered a simple message she had titled "Declaring His Glory in Suffering." Drawing on her many experiences serving in the Congo, she spoke clearly and simply about the cost of preaching the gospel, particularly in foreign lands. When she had finished, Helen was amazed at the response to her message. Large numbers of young people told her they had been challenged by her words. They also appreciated her openness and honesty as she spoke about her personal experiences. Their response made Helen wonder if becoming more involved with students might be the next step for her, though it seemed unlikely, since she was now fifty-one years old.

Helen returned to Glasgow after the Urbana conference to finish her year of volunteering with the WEC missionary college. After that she spoke at a Girls Crusader Union (GCU) summer camp in Aberlour in the north of Scotland. Helen had a long association with the Girls Crusader Union. She had run a GCU class in the garage of her parents' house in Bromley on Sunday afternoons when she was doing her medical training at West London Hospital, and many GCU groups around the country had supported her through the years. As in Urbana, Helen found a natural rapport with the girls at the summer camp.

At the end of the camp, Helen stayed with Dr. Patricia Morton and her mother. Helen had met Patricia at a previous GCU summer camp, and the two found they had much in common. Patricia was a cardiologist, interested in missions, and involved with the Girls Crusader Union. Patricia and her mother had decided to take their summer vacation in a small country hotel not too far from Aberlour. Before the first week together was over, Patricia and her mother had offered to share their home near Belfast, Northern Ireland, with Helen. They told her they would set up a bedroom for her, and that she was welcome to live with them anytime she needed a home. Helen was grateful for the gesture. Since her mother's death, she'd felt alone and a little adrift with no place to call home. Seemingly from out of nowhere, she now had a home in Ireland for as long as she needed it.

Helen was soon using the Mortons' house in Dundonald on the outskirts of Belfast as home base as she traveled to many countries representing WEC, speaking at large conventions, or sharing in small Bible studies. She continued to write books that challenged Christians to live a holy life. Yet no matter what Helen did, her time in the Congo was never far from her thoughts.

During May 1988, she received a letter from a young film director, Crawford Telfer. In his letter Crawford explained that he wanted to make a one-hour documentary on Helen's life and its impact in Africa. The documentary, which he planned to call *Mama Luka Returns*, would involve Helen's going back to all the places in the Congo that held special memories for her. The idea of the documentary excited Helen. But it also made her nervous. What would it be like to go back to those places after being away for fifteen years? Would they be the same as she remembered? Would people remember her? Or would she feel like an outsider to something she'd put so much energy into? She didn't know. While she'd kept in touch by letter with many of the locals and missionaries over the years and so had a sense of what was happening, it was one thing to write and quite another to show up in person.

Helen need not have been concerned. Several months later, when the MAF Cessna aircraft touched down on the airstrip at Nyankunde, a crowd of over one thousand people waving flowers greeted her. Inside the plane with Helen was Margaret Collingwood, an English radio personality who would be interviewing Helen and others during the trip for the documentary, along with a videography crew.

When Helen stepped out of the Cessna, she was placed into an armchair and hoisted onto the back of a pickup truck. She was driven slowly around the village, where everyone lined the streets singing and waving. Helen was overwhelmed. Everywhere she went, people hugged and fed her. She was asked to speak to many groups, and of course she was eager to find out how the medical training school was doing.

Before setting out for the Congo from England, Helen had worried about the state of her Swahili, whether she would still be able to speak the language and understand it when spoken to her. To her surprise, when she landed in Nyankunde and began interacting with the local people, Helen's Swahili came right back to her. She understood the questions being asked and knew the right words with which to reply.

Andrew Mandaboi now ran the medical training program. He was in one of the first groups of nursing students which, twenty-two years earlier, had built the rudimentary classrooms and dormitories before teaching could begin. Helen was delighted to observe Andrew teach an anatomy class. He was an excellent teacher. After graduating from the medical training school, he had gone to the University of Quebec, Canada, where he graduated with a Master of Science degree. With his degree in hand, Andrew had returned to Nyankunde, where he took over running the medical training school. Things had come full circle. This was what Helen had dreamed of—teaching Africans to take hold of their own destiny, to train and send out their own people to be medical missionaries.

While in Nyankunde, the camera crew set up their equipment and Margaret interviewed the hospital's first Congolese director, Dr. Kasereka "Jo" Lusi. In the course of the interview, he told Margaret,

> The real legacy that Dr. Roseveare has left is the school. Because wherever we go in the country and wherever we send our nurses, they all have good success and now the government is asking us to help the other [medical training] schools to [teach] exactly as [we do]. Last week the government . . . sent a commission to ask us if we could take the university doctors [and have them] come [here] and learn how to run an African Zairian hospital. . . . That is thanks to the . . . foundation we [received] from this servant of God.

That was the legacy Helen had always hoped to leave.

After several days in Nyankunde, Helen and the film crew took to the air. This time they flew to Nebobongo. At the airstrip that Helen had urged the elders to build, the entire village was lined up alongside the runway, singing and waving. The first person to greet Helen when she got out of the airplane was John Mangadima. His hair was streaked with grey now, but Helen recognized him instantly. The years fell away. She hugged John tight while he wiped the tears that streamed down his cheeks. Next Mama Damaris stepped forward, followed by Benjamin, her former house helper, who carried a bottle of water to give to Helen. Pastor Ndugu stepped up too. "Welcome home, my daughter," he said, engulfing Helen in a bear hug. She couldn't believe how tall and strong he still looked. Although she didn't know his exact age, she guessed him to be in his mid-eighties.

Helen was led to a chair, where she sat to receive the official welcome for Mama Luka. All around she could see faces she recognized. The speeches began, and then Helen was invited to a well-attended luncheon in her honor. Later Helen was given a tour of the hospital. The facility was neat and clean and served as the hub for forty-eight rural dispensaries and clinics within a fifty-mile radius. Helen couldn't have been happier. This was the plan she'd first pioneered here.

The camera crew stayed for a week in Nebobongo, filming the medical work and conducting interviews with those who'd known Helen during her time there. Every day Helen wondered if things could get any better, and they did. From Nebobongo the MAF airplane took her and the film crew to other WEC mission outposts, where Helen got to renew friendships with missionaries she'd known from her time serving in the Congo and those she had met during their furloughs back in England.

Helen's heart was full by the time she returned home. The trip had taught her two things for sure: she had been remembered, and the work she pioneered had continued on after her.

By now Helen was sixty-three years old, a respectable age to retire, but she wasn't at all interested in doing that. So much remained to be accomplished. While she was in the Congo, Pastor Ndugu had gathered a group of Christian leaders to pray for her. Much to Helen's delight, they had commissioned her to go as their missionary out into the world to preach the gospel and encourage Christians in their faith. That was what she intended to keep on doing. Speaking requests from various groups continued rolling in. Helen first went to Poland to talk to Campus Crusade workers from Eastern Europe, and then to Hong Kong to speak to one thousand teenagers. This was followed by speaking engagements in France, the United States, and Mexico. Helen even led a small group of young British women on a mission trip to Singapore and Vietnam. She led another group on a mission into several Muslim countries, which she preferred not to name for safety reasons. Everywhere she went, Helen preached the simple message that Jesus loved them and wanted them to trust Him with their lives and not falter in their faith regardless of what happened.

After Helen visited Nebobongo in 1988, she had doubted she would ever go there again. But in 2004 she was asked to return to Nebobongo to officially open a new surgical wing of the hospital. Helen, of course, jumped at the chance to see her old friends and to celebrate the wonderful addition. This time, Helen's friend and housemate Patricia accompanied her on the trip. The two women flew into Entebbe International Airport in Uganda, where an MAF airplane met them and flew them into the Congo. Helen was delighted to have Pat with her as they soared above hundreds of miles of rain forest. At last the plane dipped its wing and banked and descended toward Nebobongo, nestled on the edge of the jungle. Once more hundreds of people waited to greet Helen. It was just as exciting for her as it had been the first time.

John Mangadima was there, though this time he was no longer the hospital director. That position was now held by Dr. Mola, a Congolese physician. Shortly after her arrival, Helen promised to accompany John back to his village to see what he was doing. The people gave speeches and sang songs, some of which Helen had composed and taught to the schoolchildren when she first arrived in Nebobongo fifty years before. Now those schoolchildren were grandparents, but they still kept singing the songs.

Everyone followed Helen and Pat as they were shown around the village. The school now had seven hundred students and thirteen teachers. Most of the original mud and thatch huts had been replaced with concrete block and iron-roofed buildings.

The two women settled into the house in which Helen had lived years before. A continuous stream of friends visited Helen and met Pat there. Many of the visitors had adult children with them whom Helen had helped bring into the world. Fibi, who'd been an eight-year-old orphan when Helen took her in, was now a grandmother proudly showing off her grandchildren.

At dawn on the day they had all been waiting for, people began arriving in Nebobongo carrying all kinds of cushions and chairs to sit on. They kept coming, all six thousand of them! Many had come to witness the opening of the new surgical building while others who had heard that Mama Luka was in the village just wanted to see her.

In true African fashion, choirs sang loudly and officials gave long speeches. Helen was asked to give a word of inspiration from the Bible, which she was glad to do. Afterward she was ushered to the front of the new medical building, where a sheet hung over something to the right of the main entrance. Dr. Mola signaled for Helen to stop in front of the sheet. As he raised his hand, a schoolboy pulled on a rope. The sheet drew to the side, revealing a wooden sign that read "Surgical Center of Mama Luka." Helen burst into tears. The people had named the beautiful new building after her. That night after the official opening, everyone celebrated with feasting and music.

The following day Helen and Pat were driven to Anga, John's home village. As they rode over potholes in the pouring rain, Helen told Pat about the first time she had seen John. It was late 1953, fifty-one years ago, when John had presented himself to Helen after being fired from the Red Cross hospital in Pawa because of his Christian faith. He was the first person to ask Helen to train him, and his request had confirmed to her that she should open a medical training program. Through the program John had risen to become a first-rate nurse and surgical assistant. Then after many years away, John had returned to Anga as the local pastor.

When the group arrived at the village, Helen was amazed at what she saw. Not only was John the local pastor, but also he was the founder of a small hospital with a surgery and maternity ward, along with a secondary school with five teachers and sixty students. John had left Nebobongo and replicated its services in the jungle. Helen shook her head and smiled. John had truly learned all she had taught him.

Helen experienced other heartwarming moments during her time in and around Nebobongo that showed Helen that her legacy was still alive and strong. One of these was when she met Dr. Jean Claude Bataneni, the son of a nurse and midwife Helen had trained early on. Although Jean Claude was born after Helen left Nebobongo, he had been raised on stories about Mama Luka. He told Helen that this had inspired him to train as a doctor and that now he felt God calling him to continue his medical training in Gabon to become a surgeon. Helen prayed with him and encouraged him to take the step.

After a week of celebration at Nebobongo, Helen and Pat climbed aboard the trusty MAF Cessna airplane that would take them to Nyankunde. Helen sat quietly as she gazed at the green jungle below. She knew that the next stop was going to be difficult to take in. In September two years before, intertribal war had broken out around the hospital at Nyankunde. The violence had been triggered by the mining of gold and coltan, or columbite-tantalites, a valuable dull black metallic ore from which the elements niobium and tantalum are extracted and used in mobile phones and other electronic devices. Several nearby countries, including neighboring Rwanda and Uganda, had sent militias into northeastern Congo to take over coltan mining areas and to supply assault rifles and other weapons to two local tribes, the Lendu and the Hema, as inducements to join in the fight for resources.

On the morning of September 5, 2002, seven thousand Hema soldiers had attacked Nyankunde's hospital compound. Their faces were covered in paint, and they wore wreaths on their heads. At the hospital they shot or hacked to death over one thousand people, including patients in their beds, newborn babies, and many hospital staff, including the chaplain. Those who lived through the initial attack fled into the dense jungle. Once in the jungle, more than seven hundred doctors, nurses, and patients, some of them seriously ill, set out on foot for Oicha, 115 miles southwest, where Dr. Carl Becker had established a leper clinic many years before. Along the way several babies were born. The trek took ten days, with almost no food or water, but everyone who started out from Nyankunde arrived safely.

Helen had been devastated as she kept up with the news of what was going on in and around Nyankunde. Reports had trickled out that all the hospital buildings had been looted and then burned to the ground. Over half a million Congolese living in the area had been driven from their homes. Now it was time for Helen to see firsthand the damage to a compound that had once been a model and a beacon of hope for medical treatment in all of the Congo.

Because conflict persisted in the area, the MAF pilot was allowed only thirty minutes on the ground. This was just enough time for him to drop off supplies to the small groups that had returned to the area to start the hospital rebuilding process. Once the Cessna landed, Helen and Pat walked a well-trodden trail among the burned-out hospital complex buildings. Having been told the surrounding ground was littered with land mines, they dared not deviate from the trail. It was a heartbreaking half hour for Helen. So many memories flooded back to her: the first group of students to arrive who had doggedly built the dormitories and classrooms of the medical training facility, the worship meetings she had attended in the hospital, and the thousands of hours she'd spent helping students grasp complex medical concepts. None of it was left.

Their next stop after Nyankunde was Oicha, where Drs. Philip and Nancy Wood headed up a makeshift hospital and took responsibility for the thousands of refugees who had fled during the conflict. Helen and Pat stayed the night in Oicha, where Helen enjoyed not only the company of the couple who had taken over managing the medical training school in Nyankunde from her but also a night of fellowship with twelve of her old students.

The next day they flew on from Oicha to Beni, about twenty miles south. The students who had fled Nyankunde hospital had set up a temporary training college in Beni in some rickety warehouses. Helen and Pat were welcomed by the entire group of students, who lined up in their white uniforms and sang welcome songs. As Helen was shown around makeshift classrooms and laboratories, she felt discouraged as she thought back to the first training school at Nyankunde thirty-eight years before. For a minute she wondered why God would have allowed so many people to put so much effort into making a modern medical training facility a reality, only to have it brought so low that it was back where it had started. As the MAF Cessna took off from Beni, however, Helen realized that her thinking about the fate of the medical training school was all wrong. She often preached from the New Testament book of First Peter, chapter 2, verses 4 and 5: "Come to him, to that living stone, rejected by men but in God's sight chosen and precious; and like living stones be yourselves built into a spiritual house, to be a holy priesthood, to offer spiritual sacrifices acceptable to God through Jesus Christ" (RSV).

The medical training school was *not* back where it had started. Yes, the buildings and equipment had been destroyed, but they had never been the true aim of Helen's missionary work. The focus was the people Helen had touched, the students and patients, the living stones, those she was able to point to Jesus, who still remained unbroken by circumstances. There were so many of them: John Mangadima, with his own hospital and school in his village; Philip and Nancy Wood, who had taken over in Helen's place; Mama Damaris, who was still a vibrant Christian witness; Pastor Ndugu, who had remained faithful and true to his gospel calling; and hundreds of others who had gone through the medical training school and fanned out across the Congo, taking with them hope and healing to millions of people.

As the Cessna flew Helen and Pat back to Entebbe International Airport in Uganda, Helen thanked God that she had lived to be seventy-nine years old, long enough to see her beloved Congo one last time.

Chapter 15

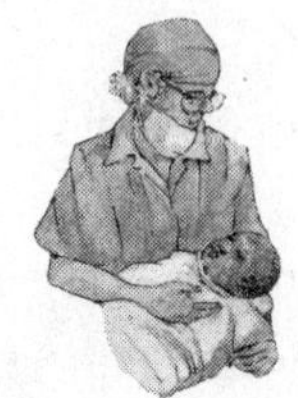

Put Jesus First

After returning from the Congo, Helen settled into semiretirement. She still accepted invitations to speak, but she also loved spending time at home in Northern Ireland studying the Bible and reading. She kept in contact with missionary friends and African Christians. She particularly enjoyed corresponding with Jean Claude Bataneni, for whom she had often prayed and to whom she had sent encouraging emails during his surgical training.

Slowly, though, Helen's health began to decline. She didn't remember things as well as she used to, and she became hard of hearing. In 2014 Helen recorded the last public video in which she spoke. The video was intended to be played at a thanksgiving gathering to be held after she died. When Helen became too frail to live at home with Patricia, she was transferred to the nearby Richmond Nursing Home, where she was lovingly cared for. She died peacefully in her bed at the nursing home on December 7, 2016, at the age of 91. Her funeral was held at her local church, St. Elizabeth's Dundonald. Besides all of the local people who attended her funeral, WEC missionaries and hundreds of others watched it via video.

During the funeral service, Dr. Nancy Wood, who with her husband, Dr. Philip Wood, had replaced Helen as head of the medical training school in Nyankunde, reported on the legacy of Helen's work in the Congo.

> I was captivated by Helen's work. She was training young men who were largely unemployed and no longer hunters and gatherers, as their tradition had been. These young men were planning to serve rural communities, which, at that time, had really only traditional medicine, which was often ineffective and sometimes fatal. . . . Not only have many of them served the Lord faithfully for a lifetime, but nine of these graduates have enabled, against all odds, to have eleven of their children go to medical school to become doctors, and four of them have completed specialist training. One of them is Dr. Jean-Claude Bataneni. He specialized in surgery for five years in Gabon and is now the medical director of Nebobongo Hospital, working with his

> wife, Dr. Christine, and four or five other GPs. One registered nurse who came to know the Lord in Nyankunde took herself off to medical school, and now Dr. Felicity heads up the AIDS prevention and treatment program for Nebobongo Hospital. Two of the nursing graduates have gone on for their PhDs. and one of them, Dr. Melchisedec Kirere, Dr. Meli for short, is the director for the Nursing College of Nyankunde in Bunia, which this year has 497 students in ten options.
>
> [The college has] eighteen full-time Congolese staff and . . . eighty-nine visiting staff. The nursing school at Nyankunde continues [with] ninety-two students this year in four options, and the nursing school of Nebobongo continues, they have 72 students this year in two options. . . . I hope from Heaven Helen can see the hundreds of people in the DRC [Democratic Republic of the Congo] who are following her example.

Three months later, at a separate thanksgiving gathering held for Helen in the large Presbyterian church in Bangor, Northern Ireland, Helen's final video was played. In the course of the video Mama Luka says,

> All of us have the privilege of being called to be His servants. It's just so wonderful. Jesus said He Himself did not come to be served

but to serve and to give, and if we have this in the back of our hearts all the time, we've not been called to some big outward thing to be written about or publicized but are called to serve Him and to serve Him because we love Him, then whatever we are doing we're doing for Jesus and for Him to be uplifted. I think that would be my major thing I would like to leave with young people today. Think in those terms: put Jesus first.

Bibliography

Abrahams, Olga Rutherford. *A Geordie in Japan*. Durham, UK: The Memoir Club, 2010.

Burgess, Alan. *Daylight Must Come: The Story of a Courageous Woman Doctor in the Congo*. New York: Delacorte Press, 1974.

Davies, David M. *The Captivity And Triumph Of Winnie Davies*. London: Hodder & Stoughton, 1968.

Grubb, Norman. *Mighty Through God: The Life of Edith Moules*. London: Lutterworth Press, 1951.

Roseveare, Helen. *Digging Ditches: The Latest Chapter of an Inspirational Life*. Fearn, UK: Christian Focus, 2005.

———. *Doctor among Congo Rebels*. London: Lutterworth Press, 1965.

———. *Doctor Returns to Congo*. London: Lutterworth Press, 1967.

———. *Give Me This Mountain: An Autobiography*. London: Inter-Varsity Press, 1966.

———. *He Gave Us a Valley*. Downers Grove, IL: Inter-Varsity Press, 1976.

Roseveare, Sir Martin. *Joys, Jobs and Jaunts: Memoirs of Sir Martin Roseveare*. Printed by the author, 1984.

About the Authors

Janet and Geoff Benge are a husband and wife writing team with more than thirty years of writing experience. Janet is a former elementary school teacher. Geoff holds a degree in history. Originally from New Zealand, the Benges spent ten years serving with Youth With A Mission. They have two daughters, Laura and Shannon, and an adopted son, Lito. They make their home in the Orlando, Florida, area.

Christian Heroes: Then & Now are available in paperback, e-book, and audiobook formats, with more coming soon!

www.YWAMpublishing.com

Also from Janet and Geoff Benge…

More adventure-filled biographies for ages 10 to 100!

Christian Heroes: Then and Now

Gladys Aylward: The Adventure of a Lifetime • 978-1-57658-019-6
Nate Saint: On a Wing and a Prayer • 978-1-57658-017-2
Hudson Taylor: Deep in the Heart of China • 978-1-57658-016-5
Amy Carmichael: Rescuer of Precious Gems • 978-1-57658-018-9
Eric Liddell: Something Greater Than Gold • 978-1-57658-137-7
Corrie ten Boom: Keeper of the Angels' Den • 978-1-57658-136-0
William Carey: Obliged to Go • 978-1-57658-147-6
George Müller: Guardian of Bristol's Orphans • 978-1-57658-145-2
Jim Elliot: One Great Purpose • 978-1-57658-146-9
Mary Slessor: Forward into Calabar • 978-1-57658-148-3
David Livingstone: Africa's Trailblazer • 978-1-57658-153-7
Betty Greene: Wings to Serve • 978-1-57658-152-0
Adoniram Judson: Bound for Burma • 978-1-57658-161-2
Cameron Townsend: Good News in Every Language • 978-1-57658-164-3
Jonathan Goforth: An Open Door in China • 978-1-57658-174-2
Lottie Moon: Giving Her All for China • 978-1-57658-188-9
John Williams: Messenger of Peace • 978-1-57658-256-5
William Booth: Soup, Soap, and Salvation • 978-1-57658-258-9
Rowland Bingham: Into Africa's Interior • 978-1-57658-282-4
Ida Scudder: Healing Bodies, Touching Hearts • 978-1-57658-285-5
Wilfred Grenfell: Fisher of Men • 978-1-57658-292-3
Lillian Trasher: The Greatest Wonder in Egypt • 978-1-57658-305-0
Loren Cunningham: Into All the World • 978-1-57658-199-5
Florence Young: Mission Accomplished • 978-1-57658-313-5
Sundar Singh: Footprints Over the Mountains • 978-1-57658-318-0
C.T. Studd: No Retreat • 978-1-57658-288-6
Rachel Saint: A Star in the Jungle • 978-1-57658-337-1
Brother Andrew: God's Secret Agent • 978-1-57658-355-5
Clarence Jones: Mr. Radio • 978-1-57658-343-2
Count Zinzendorf: Firstfruit • 978-1-57658-262-6
John Wesley: The World His Parish • 978-1-57658-382-1
C. S. Lewis: Master Storyteller • 978-1-57658-385-2
David Bussau: Facing the World Head-on • 978-1-57658-415-6
Jacob DeShazer: Forgive Your Enemies • 978-1-57658-475-0
Isobel Kuhn: On the Roof of the World • 978-1-57658-497-2
Elisabeth Elliot: Joyful Surrender • 978-1-57658-513-9
D. L. Moody: Bringing Souls to Christ • 978-1-57658-552-8
Paul Brand: Helping Hands • 978-1-57658-536-8
Dietrich Bonhoeffer: In the Midst of Wickedness • 978-1-57658-713-3
Francis Asbury: Circuit Rider • 978-1-57658-737-9
Samuel Zwemer: The Burden of Arabia • 978-1-57658-738-6

Klaus-Dieter John: Hope in the Land of the Incas • 978-1-57658-826-2
Mildred Cable: Through the Jade Gate • 978-1-57658-886-4
John Flynn: Into the Never Never • 978-1-57658-898-7
Richard Wurmbrand: Love Your Enemies • 978-1-57658-987-8
Charles Mulli: We Are Family • 978-1-57658-894-9
John Newton: Change of Heart • 978-1-57658-909-0
Helen Roseveare: Mama Luka • 978-1-57658-910-6
Norman Grubb: Mission Builder • 978-1-57658-915-1
Albert Schweitzer: Le Grand Docteur • 978-1-57658-961-8

Heroes of History

George Washington Carver: From Slave to Scientist • 978-1-883002-78-7
Abraham Lincoln: A New Birth of Freedom • 978-1-883002-79-4
Meriwether Lewis: Off the Edge of the Map • 978-1-883002-80-0
George Washington: True Patriot • 978-1-883002-81-7
William Penn: Liberty and Justice for All • 978-1-883002-82-4
Harriet Tubman: Freedombound • 978-1-883002-90-9
John Adams: Independence Forever • 978-1-883002-50-3
Clara Barton: Courage under Fire • 978-1-883002-51-0
Daniel Boone: Frontiersman • 978-1-932096-09-5
Theodore Roosevelt: An American Original • 978-1-932096-10-1
Douglas MacArthur: What Greater Honor • 978-1-932096-15-6
Benjamin Franklin: Live Wire • 978-1-932096-14-9
Christopher Columbus: Across the Ocean Sea • 978-1-932096-23-1
Laura Ingalls Wilder: A Storybook Life • 978-1-932096-32-3
Orville Wright: The Flyer • 978-1-932096-34-7
Captain John Smith: A Foothold in the New World • 978-1-932096-36-1
Thomas Edison: Inspiration and Hard Work • 978-1-932096-37-8
Alan Shepard: Higher and Faster • 978-1-932096-41-5
Ronald Reagan: Destiny at His Side • 978-1-932096-65-1
Davy Crockett: Ever Westward • 978-1-932096-67-5
Milton Hershey: More Than Chocolate • 978-1-932096-82-8
Billy Graham: America's Pastor • 978-1-62486-024-9
Ben Carson: A Chance at Life • 978-1-62486-034-8
Louis Zamperini: Redemption • 978-1-62486-049-2
Elizabeth Fry: Angel of Newgate • 978-1-62486-064-5
William Wilberforce: Take Up the Fight • 978-1-62486-057-7
William Bradford: Plymouth's Rock • 978-1-62486-092-8
Ernest Shackleton: Going South • 978-1-62486-093-5
Benjamin Rush: The Common Good • 978-1-62486-123-9
Dwight Eisenhower: Supreme Commander • 978-1-62486-142-0
Frederick Douglass: The Right to Dignity • 978-1-62486-151-2
Winston Churchill: Resolute • 978-1-62486-153-6

Heroes of History
GEORGE WASHINGTON
True Patriot
JANET & GEOFF BENGE

Heroes of History
GEORGE WASHINGTON
True Patriot
JANET & GEOFF BENGE
Emerald Books

Heroes of History
Audio Heroes
GEORGE WASHINGTON
True Patriot
JANET & GEOFF BENGE

Heroes of History
HARRIET TUBMAN
Freedombound
JANET & GEOFF BENGE

Heroes of History
HARRIET TUBMAN
Freedombound
JANET & GEOFF BENGE
Emerald Books

Heroes of History
Audio Heroes
HARRIET TUBMAN
Freedombound
JANET & GEOFF BENGE